"*Beirut Fragments,* like a eulogy, staggers sharply down Beirut's bombed-out streets, pausing for moments of doleful lyricism, numbness, and rage.... What distinguishes *Beirut Fragments* from other writing about Beirut is that Makdisi... tracks the war's devastation not as a journalist but as a Beiruti who is forcing a lacy compromise between personal memoir and modern history.... an angry and sometimes hopeful homage to the Beirutis who stayed despite the exponential carnage."

—*The Village Voice*

"[A] beautifully crafted memoir... the first detailed account by a civilian of daily life in the cockpit of the Middle East war."

—*Publishers Weekly*

"Makdisi skillfully weaves history with personal experience to produce a work ringing with truth and insight which appeals to the reader's intellect and understanding while evoking compassion for all those who have refused to give up on Beirut and in so doing have created a testimonial to the resiliency of the human spirit as well as to the wastefulness, wantonness, and randomness of war."

—*Arab Book World*

"[A] rare insider's view of a tragic and protracted conflict."

—*Kirkus Reviews*

"Beirut at last has found its biographer. Jean Said Makdisi's uncommonly perceptive and deeply moving account of the city's agony reveals the human side of Beirut's tragedy. She deliberately avoids the 'political' dimension, and yet she has presented a profound indictment of the inhuman politics of this conflict."

—Michael C. Hudson, Professor of International Relations and Government, Center for Contemporary Arab Studies, Georgetown University

(continued on next page)

Beirut Fragments

A WAR MEMOIR

Jean Said Makdisi

PERSEA BOOKS NEW YORK

For information, write to the publisher:
Persea Books, Inc.
60 Madison Avenue
New York, New York 10010

Library of Congress Cataloging in Publication Data
Makdisi, Jean Said.
Beirut fragments; a war memoir / Jean Said Makdisi.
p.   cm.
ISBN 0-89255-164-X
1. Lebanon—History—1975– 2. Makdisi, Jean Sadi. 3. Beirut
(Lebanon)—Description. I. Title.
DS87.M355   1989   89-26533
956.9204'4—dc 20   CIP

Portions of this book have previously appeared,
in somewhat different form, in *Wigwag, Harper's, The New York Review of Books,*
and *Raritan: A Quarterly Review.*

Designed by REM Studio, Inc.
Set in Stempel Garamond by The Studley Press, Inc., Dalton, Massachusetts
Printed and bound by Haddon Craftsmen, Scranton, Pennsylvania
First paperback printing

Dedicated to Beirut and its long-suffering people,
who, in spite of everything, have kept its spirit alive,

and especially to Samir,
who taught me what that spirit means.

Contents

[7]

Beirut
Fragments

CHRONOLOGY

April 13, 1975. A series of local and regional developments lead to the sparking incident of the war in a Beirut suburb. Battles between the PLO and the Kataeb (Phalange) Christian militia later spread to other parts of Beirut, especially the downtown area which is totally destroyed and eventually becomes part of the demarcation line between the two parts of the city. Many militias are formed on both sides. Hundreds of civilians are killed or taken hostage. The Lebanese government is divided, and later the army is split behind the warring factions. The militias gradually usurp many functions of the state.

January, 1976. A ferocious battle is fought in the slum of Karantina, which falls to the Kataeb. Later in the month, the Christian town of Damour is sacked in retaliation. In both places, scores of civilians are killed and the remnants evicted.

May, 1976. The Parliament elects a new president, Elias Sarkis.

Summer, 1976. A great battle in the Palestinian refugee camp of Tal-el-Zaatar ends with the defeat of the PLO forces there. Again, scores of civilians are killed and the rest evicted. The Syrian army intervenes directly in Lebanon for the first time.

October, 1976. A ceasefire called by a summit meeting of Arab states in Riyadh, Saudi Arabia, is backed in November by the arrival of peacekeeping troops from Syria, Sudan,

Yemen, and Saudi Arabia. Later, all the Arab forces, except for the Syrians, will withdraw.

February, 1978. A clash occurs between the Syrian and Lebanese armies at Fayadieh, and the truce collapses. Fighting resumes everywhere, with the PLO controlling the south of the country and the border with Israel, as well as West Beirut. Syria maintains its presence in Beirut and controls the Bekaa valley and the north.

March, 1978. A major Israeli incursion into the south ends with the deployment of United Nations troops on the Lebanese-Israeli border. Fighting continues in Beirut and elsewhere in the country. Militias on both sides are backed by various foreign powers, including Israel which sets up the South Lebanon Army.

February, 1979. The Iranian revolution takes place and helps radicalize part of the Shiite movement in Lebanon.

July, 1980. Bashir Gemayel, leader of the Kataeb militia, unites all the Christian militias by force, naming his new coalition the Lebanese Forces.

Summer, 1982. The Israelis invade Lebanon and lay seige to West Beirut. Syrian troops withdraw from Beirut. In late August, PLO troops are evacuated under the supervision of troops from the United States, France, Great Britain, and Italy, who then depart.

The Parliament meets on August 23 and elects Bashir Gemayel president. On September 14, Bashir Gemayel is assassinated, and Israeli troops move into West Beirut where hundreds of Palestinian civilians in the refugee camps of Sabra and Shatila are massacred by members of the Lebanese Forces undeterred by the Israelis. The multinational troops return to protect the camps and to keep the peace. The Israelis withdraw from Beirut. The Parliament meets again on September 22 and elects Bashir's brother, Amin Gemayel, president.

During the Israeli occupation of Beirut, armed resistance to their presence begins which will later move to the south.

April, 1983. The United States embassy in West Beirut is blown up. Press reports claim an important CIA meeting was in progress.

Summer, 1983. The Israelis withdraw from the Shouf mountains, and heavy fighting ensues between the Lebanese Forces and the Druse militia, the Progressive Socialist Party, which results in a mass exodus of Christians from the region. During the fighting, many towns are destroyed on both sides and hundreds of civilians killed, especially in the Christian town of Bhamdoun.

October, 1983. The United States and French marines headquarters are blown up, resulting in hundreds of casualties.

February, 1984. The Lebanese army, which has been in control of Beirut since the Israeli withdrawal, is expelled from West Beirut, accused of partisanship with the Lebanese Forces, mass arrests, etc. That part of the army which remains proves ineffective in maintaining order. Militias, especially the Shiite Amal and the Druse Progressive Socialist Party, take over control of West Beirut. The multi-national forces withdraw from Lebanon. Battles among the militias in West Beirut occur over the next few years.

February, 1985. The Israelis withdraw from Sidon, but remain in the south. Armed resistance to Israeli occupation intensifies, while fighting southeast of Sidon leads to the evacuation of Christian villages there. The first armed demonstration of Hezbollah, which is backed by Iran, takes place in the predominantly Shiite, southern suburb of Beirut.

October, 1985. A massive car bomb in the southern suburb of Beirut, directed at the spiritual leader of Hezbollah, Sheik Fadlallah, is blamed on the CIA. Many of the huge car bombs and political assassinations that periodically shake the city are popularly attributed to "the intelligence services war" between the many countries involved in Lebanon.

February, 1987. At the request of the authorities in West Beirut, the Syrian army intervenes once again to put a stop to the anarchy and street fighting among the militias. Heavy fighting later begins between Amal and Hezbollah.

December, 1987. As the Intifada begins on the West Bank and in Gaza, the resistance to Israeli occupation in south Lebanon continues. It includes civilian protest and armed attacks by leftist, nationalist, and Muslim groups. By now the Israelis have imprisoned hundreds of Lebanese and Palestinians, whose release is among the demands of those holding Western hostages in Beirut.

September, 1988. As the term of President Amin Gemayel expires, Parliament fails to elect a new president. In his last official action, Gemayel appoints the commander of the army, General Michel Aoun, as interim prime minister. Neither Aoun nor his government is recognized by the authorities in West Beirut, where what is left of the former cabinet continues to govern.

February, 1989. After a battle with the Lebanese Forces, General Aoun closes their illegal ports and wrests control of the

Port of Beirut from them. He blockades the illegal ports in West Beirut and the south.

March 14, 1989. General Aoun declares war on the Syrian presence in Lebanon. Seven months of cross-town shelling end with a ceasefire negotiated by the Arab League.

October, 1989. The Lebanese Parliament meets in Taif, Saudi Arabia and negotiates a settlement of the conflict, including political reforms and a schedule for the withdrawal of Syrian troops from the country.

November, 1989. The Parliament meets again in Koleiat, in North Lebanon, ratifies the Taif accord, and elects René Moawad president. Shortly before, in an action which is widely viewed as outside the bounds of legality, Aoun dissolves Paraliament. He rejects the Taif accord and denies the legitimacy of Moawad's election. The international community, including the great powers, recognizes Moawad, who is also backed by most domestic parties.

November 22, 1989. President Moawad is assassinated. Within a few days the Parliament elects Elias Hrawi president. As before, General Aoun denies the legitimacy of Parliament's action. Hrawi forms a government, and a new commander of the army is appointed.

January 30, 1990. Heavy fighting begins in the eastern region between that part of the Lebanese army which is still under the command of General Aoun and the Lebanese Forces. As the battles rage on, the Lebanese Forces acknowledge the legitimacy of the Hrawi government. In the meantime, sporadic fighting continues between Amal and Hezbollah. Resistance to the Israeli occupation also continues, as do Israeli reprisal raids.

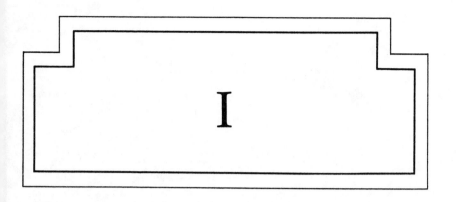

I

Prologue

HOW can I write about Beirut? How can I collect it all into one volume: the years of pain; of watching a world collapse while trying to stave off that collapse; the layers of memories and hopes, of tragedy and even sometimes comedy, of violence and kindness, of courage and fear?

Above all, how can I express my strange love for this mutilated city; how to explain, both to myself and to others, the lingering magic of the place that has kept me and and so many others clinging to its wreckage, refusing to let go, refusing to abandon it? I feel today, after fifteen years of war, more attached, more committed to Beirut than ever, even dependent on it in a strange sort of way, like a suckling child toward its mother. This commitment has something to do with loyalty;

with faith in a better future; with solidarity with those who could not leave, especially a generation of students trapped in the war and with all those who have also committed themselves to keep the place alive. But it is also based in anger, in a kind of furious defense of the collective humanity so outraged in Beirut.

As the violence reached paroxysm after paroxysm—and the world watched with indifference, or, at best, revulsion, even while feeding it with more weapons—I have felt as much impatience with that world as anger at invading armies, local warlords and anonymous car bombers. Outsiders look at Beirut from a wary distance, as though it had nothing to do with them; as though, through a protective glass partition, they were watching with immunity a patient thrash about in mortal agony, suffering a ghastly virus contracted in forbidden and faraway places. They speak of Beirut as if it were an aberration of the human experience: It is not. Beirut was a city like any other and its people were a people like any other. What happened here could, I think, happen anywhere.

From the inside, I watched and I recorded. I wrote to master that experience which was consuming me and the world in which I lived. I wrote as a witness to the common experiences of common people, feeling that in the trial of history there should be a record, a vindication, of their pain. I wrote secretly at first, but as more people learned that I was writing and recording, they would tell me, "Put that in your book," or "Tell them about that"—something that had happened to them, but about which the outside world hadn't seemed to care. Sharing that pain, and writing about it, I came to love the place. Writing about Beirut, I attached myself to it—for I am not a native Beiruti, but a wandering person—and made it mine, and myself part of it. Now every inch of that shattered city is mine. I have earned my place in the world.

When the war began I belonged everywhere and nowhere, one of a breed of human beings so common in modern times, who have moved from place to place, adjusting their papers with their peregrinations. My family came originally from Palestine, but I grew up in Egypt as an outsider. I was educated by Englishmen and Americans, absorbing their culture and values along with those handed down by my own Arab ancestors. I was tossed about in the gales the two worlds blew at each other. I married a Lebanese firmly rooted in Arab culture. We lived in America for many years and then we went to Beirut. He was returning home, and I thought that in going with him I could attach myself to his firm roots. But the vine does not share the roots of the oak: It grows its own, and so have I now. My roots are entangled in the ambiguities and contradictions of the war in Lebanon.

When the war began, I had young children, and was prepared only for the sheltered life of women of my generation. In my spare time, I had started to teach the odd course at a university founded by American Protestant missionaries decades ago, and the ambiguities of its ancestry provided, in the context of the cultural dimension of the war, an added burden. As my children grew, I had to defend them from one life-threatening situation after another, and the war imposed more and more responsibilities on me and other women. The crises of the war were often ones which fell into the traditional realm of women. We had to provide domestic supplies, deal with wrecked homes, create alternative shelters, cope with death. Women, protected by tradition from such practices as kidnapping, often found themselves directly confronting the violence that their men eschewed. Women grew in the war.

My husband, Samir, also a professor, turned down offer after offer to leave the country and work abroad, and I supported his choice. As people left in ever-increasing numbers, those of us who stubbornly remained took on wider responsibilities. Our work in the universities became more important even as it became more difficult and complicated. As all this happened, and as I wrote, a new woman grew up in me, and my skin molted.

The question remained, however, how to write, what

form to choose. I tried to force the experience into a comprehensible shape. I searched for a form to fit it into, for some implement to help me impose my need for order on the chaos around me, and I found instead that the chaos imposed itself on me. Clarity, reason, justice, symmetry, tradition, decorum—those were the tools I brought and they were as easily defeated as if I had tried to contain a pool of blood with a picket fence. Forms defaulted one by one as I held them up for trial against a crumbling reality. I wanted something uniform to hold it all, for I am one person—am I not?—and my need for unity and exactness grew in proportion as the country about me fell further and further apart.

I thought at first I should keep a diary. I wish that I had. The first time my home was shelled, March 22, 1976, might perhaps have been described like this:

> *Hardly slept last night. Battles in the hotel district undiminished. Heard new sounds. Thought battles closer than usual. Drank a lot of coffee this morning, trying to clear my mind. Everyone fidgets. No school for the children. Decide to clean the house— good therapy for tired nerves. Start dusting. The maid, K, is not at all helpful; keeps wringing her hands and peering out of the window. Send children downstairs to play, as they are getting on my nerves with their quarrels and demands. Where is my husband?*
>
> *Suddenly there is a tremendous crash. Glass all around me shatters. Fragments everywhere. No time to think what has happened. Clatter on staircase and voices. Run to the door. Neighbors running down the stairs. "Get down to the garage," someone yells at me. "Yallah, yallah, hurry up," I call to K, who is in hysterics, shaking visibly as she makes the sign of the cross over and over and calls loudly, "Ya Adra, O*

Virgin, Ya Adra." Push her outside and lead her downstairs, stopping only to collect my keys.

Collect children from playground, where I see to my relief Samir has turned up too, and all of us go to underground parking lot. Everyone is there, some still in pajamas, milling around. What happened? What was that? Another tremendous crash. General hysteria. "That was close." Another crash. The building shakes. "Closer." "Get away from the entrance." "Get away from the boiler." "Turn off the boiler." "Turn off the electricity." It goes dark.

Shaking more than ever and still making the sign of the cross, still calling to the Virgin, K sets up an altar in the corner near one of the cars and kneels down in frantic prayer. Now the concierge of the building suddenly becomes hysterical. Having ushered his wife and children into the garage, he runs upstairs and produces a Kalashnikov, which he is now brandishing wildly. "I'm going to kill them," he screams, "I'm going to kill them! They are going to kill us all!" The other men surround and gradually overpower him, yelling at him to shut up. They disarm him, and abashed, he suddenly subsides and sits in a corner with hung head, clutching, instead of the Kalashnikov, his youngest child, who is howling.

Children all want to go to the bathroom. (If truth be told, so does everyone else). No bathroom to go to. Create a pissoir in a corner; the little boys enjoy themselves briefly with their rival streams. I catch the eye of MS who looks at me sheepishly and shrugs his shoulders. Last night, over a drink, he had carefully analyzed the political and military situation and had proved beyond any doubt, to his own and his listeners' total satisfaction, that no matter what happened anywhere in Beirut, our area was absolutely safe.

Newspapermen at garage entrance. TV cameras. "We want to go upstairs to take pictures." They are turned away. We come to the quite false conclusion that there is battle in the nearby U.S. embassy (the only logical place for a battle near us) and since ours is a conspicuously high building, that the newsmen would find it convenient to cover the battle from our roof. It isn't until much later that we understand why, in fact, they have come.

New excitement. A friend who lives down the street has turned up in the garage, gesticulating madly. "There is a huge hole on the side of your building, on the sixth floor," she pants. "I came to see if you were all right." Sixth floor empty: The American tenants had packed up and gone away weeks ago. LB runs upstairs to inspect the premises, in spite of her husband's remonstrances and comes back irritated. "Nonsense," she says firmly. "There is nothing wrong with the sixth floor. People exaggerate so."

A quick conference. Wherever the battle, we may be pinned down for hours, or for days. We should go upstairs in this calm to bring down provisions. One delegate for each flat. Be sure not to use the lift. I climb the seven flights to my flat, scared but exhilarated by the excitement and glad to have a break, however dangerous, from my clinging, frightened children.

Front door doesn't open. Wrong keys? After a little struggle, lock gives way. I have an impression of total whiteness. Strange, I think to myself, when did Samir have time to cover everything with white sheets? Funny: I don't own enough white sheets to cover everything. Funny: Why did he move the piano to the middle of the room before covering it, and why did he push the great heavy chest that decorates the entrance hall into the corridor?

I look into the dining room. Good God! One of L's paintings has fallen from upstairs into my dining room. How can that be? Another look. That's no painting from upstairs. That is a hole, a great, gaping hole. I am looking at policemen, who are looking at me through the hole in the wall. They are standing on the roof of the police station next door, staring in my direction.

Realization dawns. Those are not white sheets, but dust. The place is a shambles. Everything is white and broken. Real fear now. This is death. Not something to be read about in the newspapers, but something that has come into my house, that has violated my life, my territory, my being. I walk into the bedrooms, hardly able to keep my balance, as the floor is covered unevenly with inches of rubble. Pick up a few things, a teddy bear off the floor, a blanket draped over a lamp, someone's dusty pajamas. There is no logic to what I collect.

On the way out I pick up a piece of shrapnel from the rubble. Shrapnel. So this is shrapnel, I think. I never took it seriously before. Somehow when I had heard someone had died of shrapnel wounds, it hadn't sounded quite as serious as dying from a bullet or in a fire. But this jagged, heavy, twisted, hot piece of iron—this is shrapnel. Shrapnel is serious.

I rush downstairs, trembling. I can't wait to tell everyone. It's the seventh floor, the seventh, not the sixth. More people have gathered in the garage. My voice must be very small. No one is listening. I have to tug at elbows to get attention. Finally everyone is gathered around me, not quite believing my story. Some dash upstairs to see for themselves and return as white as the sight they have seen.

Now it all makes sense. The newsmen had come to record a new stage in the war. The army has split:

For the first time they are using big guns against each other—155mm artillery. Ours is the first home to be hit.

I could never have written that on the day it happened. I was too frightened—more frightened than I have ever been before or since—too shaken, too disoriented. I did not have a notebook. It was lost in the rubble somewhere. I was too busy calming the children and trying to settle down in my mother's house, where we had to move. The thing matured in my mind only after having been recounted over and over again. One neighbor told me later—I do not believe him—that I was crying when I announced my discovery that morning. Another congratulated me on my bravery and stoicism. I like that much better.

Part of the trouble with a diary is that it limits one to one's personal experience or that it reduces vast events to small anecdotes, for that is often how vast events are experienced. What, indeed, are vast events but ones that affect a great number of people, whose individually insignificant tales may appear pathetic or comical, but rarely grand? Thus I might have recorded in my diary the collapse of an entire society by recounting a series of episodes centered, for example, around car thefts.

The first perception many people had that their world was in mortal danger came from apparently unimportant troubles. The early battles were distant, faraway events that were dismissed as irrelevant by those not directly involved. But when a plague of car thefts afflicted this relatively crime-free city, people sat up and took bewildered notice. I recorded a scene my friend W, very early on in the war, told me with hilarious sadness. She was standing on the balcony of her flat on Hamra Street one afternoon, and saw an elegant car driven by an elegant woman with another elegant woman by her side. The car broke down just in front of W's house, and no matter what the driver did, would not start, leaving her flustered and help-less. A dapper young man walked up and volunteered his assistance. Gratefully, the women got out of the car and handed it over to his ministrations. A policeman and several passersby gathered around offering friendly advice. After tin-kering under the hood for a few minutes, the young man climbed into the driver's seat. Sticking his head out of the window, he suggested politely to the small crowd that they push the car to give it a start. In comradely spirit, everyone joined in the endeavor, shoulder to shoulder: policeman, ele-gant ladies, and all. Sure enough, the car started, and, as the group watched, amazement preceding outrage on their faces, the young man and the car disappeared down the street, never to return.

Soon no one could leave a car on the streets without running the risk of losing it. With insurance no longer available and the police increasingly powerless, a brisk business grew up of reselling cars to their rightful owners. You would go to the center of the trade in Baalbek, far away from the reach of what little government authority was left. There you would be greeted by the redoubtable Abu Shawki, who would accord friendly hospitality, offering cigarettes, coffee, or a cold drink. You would then be escorted around the great parking lot to pick out your own car, showing papers to prove ownership, and then pay whatever fee Abu Shawki saw fit to charge. A friend of ours paid 10,000 pounds for his 50,000 pound car and drove it home, deeming himself lucky to have found it at all.

Once we heard a story that, whatever the facts, could easily have been true, as it was believed and as it so well reflected the utter lunacy of those days. A man had gone to the bank and withdrawn a large sum of money with which he intended to pay his employees, placing it in a briefcase. On his way home, he had to stop somewhere for a few minutes, and, calculating that he ran a heavier risk of losing his briefcase than having his car stolen he locked the briefcase into the trunk.

Returning to his parking place he found, to his horror, that the car had disappeared. He made his pilgrimage to Abu Shawki, found his car, and fearing to mention the briefcase, peered into the trunk. Abu Shakwki noted his crestfallen look when he saw that the trunk was empty and indignantly scolded him. "You are looking for your money and you think we took it?" he bellowed. "What do you take us for, thieves? *Wallaw*! Is there no trust left in this world? What has the country come to?" The man was ushered, astonished, into an office where the briefcase was produced and where he was exhorted to count the money. A little charade was played out. Feigning absolute trust, he refused to count the cash: Abu Shawki insisted. Again and again he refused, itching to find out, and again and again Abu Shawki insisted, each time more vehemently. Finally and reluctantly, he gave way and found, to his even greater astonishment, that the money was intact, down to the last pound. Becoming adept, he took up the charade again and insisted on sharing part of the sum with Abu Shawki who, feigning horror at the thought, but gun firmly and visibly on hip, refused. Repeatedly he insisted until, as a special favor, Abu Shawki relented and accepted a sizable contribution, explaining that he could not bear to injure his guest's feelings by maintaining his refusal.

Such vignettes tell more about the realities of Beirut life than the reams of newspaper articles with their interminable political analyses and predictions, most of which prove, sooner or later, to be quite wrong. The signs of societal breakdown were not, of course, limited to car thefts. For instance, one particularly painful tale involved Spinney's, a huge modern supermarket patronized by the grandes dames of Beirut but situated near the notorious "poverty belt" surrounding the city. In the initial euphoria of anarchy, it naturally became the first target of looters, most of whom, of course, had never seen the inside of the place before. One unfortunate man triumphantly carried off a whole shelf of cans, only to discover when he got home that his treasure was composed entirely of cat food. "Cat food!" he was said to have yelled to the more literate neighbor who made the discovery, "Cat food! They make food for cats? I thought we could live on this for weeks, and it is only good for cats?"

Later, Beirutis were no longer surprised by such stories and came to describe incidents with a wry and contemptuous tone, overlaid on the patient humor that for years, they had marshaled to help offset what they had to bear. For instance, six years into the war, the number of extant militias was augmented by one more—wearing uniforms of a deep, striking pink. The favorite parlor game for a while was finding an appropriate name for the pink militia, every new entry making the rounds to hilarious applause. Thus, "The Pink Panthers," "The Pink Brigades," and "The Pink Army" were entered, but judgment was finally given by consensus to "Die Rosen-kavaliere," the elegance and sophistication of that name in supreme contrast with those men slouching around in the sun in their pink uniforms.

For years a balance between horror and ordinary life was maintained. For example, the St. Simon was, before the war, an exclusive beach club on whose yellow sands lolled the beautiful people of Beirut. Then, after one of the bloodiest battles of the war, the remnants of the slum community of Karantina, on the other side of the city, arrived in truckloads and took refuge there. The changing cabins, with their flow-ered shower curtains and striped canvas deck chairs, plus small refrigerators for chilling beer and soda, became houses to whole families; and the place was converted overnight from a luxurious playground to a slum. Soon after the first phase of the war ended in 1976 a new beach club opened next door, complete with potted geraniums, white reclining chairs, artifi-cial waterfalls, lawns, tennis courts, saunas, health clubs, and beauty shops. Summerland, it was boasted, rivaled the most exclusive beaches in the south of France.

Then, one day, a car bomb emploded near the St. Simon beach. No sooner had the procession of ambulances carried away the human debris—the wailing sirens accompanied by volleys of gunfire to clear the road, by screams of panic and mourning and despair—than another procession of cars started arriving at Summerland. The YWCA Green Thumb Club was holding its annual spring flower show. This year's festivities took the form of a historical fashion show: A parade of bridal gowns from 1900 to the present was applauded, each model carrying a bouquet characteristic of an epoch.

I once envisaged a whole book of such tales but gave up the idea. There is something offensive and skewed about concentrating on the underbelly of the monster War. It leaves out the monster's familiar face. How to relate those awesome events that are not reducible to anecdote? "Heard today about the latest horror. Hundreds of people were killed in—" (Name the place, it has happened often enough.)

Just when one thinks that the war is over, that, for better or worse, one has understood what it was all about, that one knows, to borrow the vulgar Lebanese phrase, on which stake one has been impaled; just as one gets one's political bearings after emerging from the bomb shelter in the latest battle, and, looking around, blaming this or that faction for its arrogance, shortsightedness, cruelty, and treacherous alliance with this or that foreign power; just then the whole picture changes again. A new battle erupts, and new political realities appear. It is like looking through a kaleidoscope: Shake it, and a design appears; shake it again, and an altogether different one replaces it. Shifts happened so often that one wonders if they will ever end, or, if they do, if one will recognize the end, having long ago despaired of reaching it.

Should I write with hope? The guns are silent; the blood has stopped flowing. Handshakes have been exchanged, agreements arrived at. The dead have been buried, the exiles have returned.

Shake the kaleidoscope. The guns have re-erupted; blood is flowing again. Should I write with despair?

Shake the kaleidoscope.

Bitter humor? Black anger? Denunciation? Irony? Sorrow?

Symbolism? But the street that symbolized one group's triumph yesterday is the symbol of its rival's triumph today. The town that was once symbolic of this people's sorrow, has now become their enemy's burial ground. Yesterday's allies are today's enemies; yesterday's enemies are in close conference today. Yesterday's hero has become today's villain, and yesterday's villain, today's martyr.

In the early days of the war, I wrote the occasional essay spontaneously and effortlessly. I wrote more than one piece entitled "The Morning After an Israeli Air-Raid," and then modifed the title to "The Morning after Another Israeli Air-Raid," and then, "The Morning after yet another Israeli Air-Raid—Five Years Later." As time went on, anger and pain grew far beyond the bonds that mere essay could contain, and then it seemed that only satire, which turns reason and logic inside out in response to a world gone mad, could deal with the problem. But that, too, proved insufficient.

I plumbed the most morbid recesses of my imagination to find a metaphor or image capable of expressing some of the pain of Beirut, and then I watched in horror as that vision turned into bloody, unspeakable reality. Years ago, I wrote a piece entitled "Nightmare." I imagined myself walking down a crowded street scattered with the garbage which scars the city, in one of the traffic jams which interminably plague us, and then I imagined an explosion and a hideous scramble of cars, garbage, and multilated bodies. That was before the numbing series of car bombings on crowded streets became an integral part of our lives, and my nightmare vision became indistinguishable from straightforward reporting. All the drives and dreams of a universal id seem to have come alive in Beirut and have been translated into physical reality. There are no dreams left here; it is no longer possible to dream.

In Beirut, our eyes are fixed open with the white tape of violence so that the distinction between night and day, dream and reality, is lost. All I can do is set down what I have seen, my glimpses into the heart of violence and madness, of a society being—dismembered? constructed? reconstructed? destroyed? resurrected?—*changed*. I can do no more than that.

II

Crisis,
with Glossary
of Terms Used in
Times of Crisis

I T is a beautiful evening. From the balcony of my flat near the American University of Beirut, I watch the sun sink into the calm blue waters of the Mediterranean. The red-tiled roofs of the older buildings on campus, among the last left in this once beautiful city, and the dark green grace of the cypress trees gradually lose their distinctive contrast as the sun rays fade away and the city lights come on. To the east, the deep purple of the distant hills above Jounieh modulate into a serene blackness, and the sparkle of village and automobile lights reflect the stars in the night sky. The clock on the tower above College Hall strikes, and the chimes die away into the quiet evening. Often I stand, as I do tonight, listening, thinking, of how those same chimes have rung over the decades, when a clock was just a clock, not a bell tolling for a dying city and a dying time. Somehow the thought is comforting though infinitely sad.

Suddenly, the quiet catches my ear. With that sixth sense that Beirutis have developed, I go inside and turn on the ubiquitous radio. Martial music blares out at me, and my heart sinks. Another crisis. Where? Who is fighting whom this time? I go out to the other balcony, the one facing the city, where, as I expected, the white stars fade in the light of the red tracer bullets; the quiet of the evening is broken by the too-familiar sound of guns. They call to my mind drums in the jungle, a primitive, ritual warning of aggression and danger.

Dread and excitement churn in my stomach. The normalcy of the last few months since the last crisis fades into nightmare; everything that we have done in calm moments seems to have been a postponement of eventualities. It is as though we have been on a fragile craft in the middle of the ocean, drifting along, dreamily watching the sharks swim by, contemplating the nature of things. When the gale approaches, the craft trembles, and fear takes hold. Yet it is the gale that will take us to shore. It may kill us on the way, but the risk is preferable to the drifting towards certain death.

As I wait for the news bulletin, I take nervous mental stock of things: First, a quick survey of the whereabouts of my family—all present and accounted for—and then another of supplies. There is a strange and sudden loud whistle outside, followed by a tremendous crash as the first shell lands nearby. I quickly take down the bag containing passports, identity papers, what cash is on hand. My husband comes in and we have a brief consultation. Should we call the children and go downstairs to the garage shelter? "Let's wait a while," he says. We're on our own. It's each family for itself; each makes its own fateful decision. There is no guide and no help. There are no warning sirens, only those of ambulances after the fact. If you go down too soon, you may look foolish; if you don't go down soon enough, you may die.

The children rush in. They look at our faces to see how scared they should be. The sight of the emergency bag that I have hastily packed creates excitement. "No school tomorrow?" asks my worldly eldest. It occurs to me that the children rather enjoy these crises, that is, until true terror strikes. Everyone is at home; having become thoroughly irrelevant, discipline collapses. No one is told to be quiet and do his homework. Bedtime is any time and no time. Daddy, one ear on the radio, the other on the noise outside, will indulgently if absentmindedly agree to play a game in an inside room to try to fight off their fear.

Another tremendous crash follows the whiz of a shell, and the windows rattle. I tear around the house opening all the windows, remembering the time I hadn't and the glass had to be replaced. My husband and I exchange glances as another set of footsteps clatters down the stairs. The phone rings. It is my mother. "Where is your sister?" she asks, almost hysterical. "That girl will be the death of me. She said she was going to . . ." The line dies. "The phone is dead," I inform my husband. The lights flicker, and I clutch the flashlight in my pocket.

Another crash outside and my husband stands up. "Okay. Let's go." The children pick up things they consider necessary. One collects his comic books, another his hamster in its cage. "Put that thing back," I say, too loudly. "I will not go without him." "For heaven's sake, put that cage back and let's go." "I won't go without him." Another crash. The lights go off. "Okay, okay. Let's go."

We stumble down the dark stairs into the garage, as we have done so often. Each time we sit in the excruciating discomfort we swear that next week we are going to improve the shelter, have matresses and lights ready and the all-important toilet, but somehow we never do. My youngest son reiterates the question about school tomorrow. He hugs me in apparent cheerfulness, but I can feel the pounding of his heart.

For hours, the sounds outside are frightful but gradually

recede into the distance. When it becomes clear that the shelling is no longer directed at our part of the city, people start leaving the garage. We get the children to bed, all together in one room. They refuse to undress, and I make sure that their shoes are easily accessible. I have to sit by them, patting them and singing and telling stories until they are calm enough to go to sleep.

By then, of course, I am thoroughly exhausted, but far too nervous to sleep myself. I join my husband on the balcony, and in silence we watch the flares and rockets falling on the city. There is nothing to be said; only the imagination works now on those families who are still in their underground garages, in those quarters where the shells are landing. By around two in the morning everything is quiet and we finally doze off, only to be awakened again later by distant shelling.

The day starts later. The noise of battle has subsided. A new ceasefire has gone into effect. We resume our normal rounds. My husband startles me by saying that the children should get ready for school. "School," I say, "school? Are you mad?" "We'll let them go. If there is no school they will come back." "But the streets—" "There is nothing here, *ma fi shi*." Reluctantly, I tell the even more reluctant children to get ready for school. They go; they come back. "No school," they yell, flinging their satchels to the floor and running to spread the glad tidings among their playmates in the building.

My husband is at the door. "Where are you going?" "I'll be in the office if you need me." "Please don't go. What if—" He waves away my question. "You can't live like that." It's true: you can't. The *what ifs* can only be waved away. The inconceivable is bearable only if it remains unconceived, so until the inconceivable happens we wave it away. Maybe next time it will be my turn; until then I will carry on.

I get dressed and knock at my neighbor's door. All the children are there. "I have to go to work," I announce timorously, looking to see if she thinks I am as mad as I do. "You're going?" Her words form not so much a question as a comment. "Well, what can I do? We have to carry on," I answer defensively, sick of the words and wondering why we keep saying them—and whether they are true. "If anything should happen—" nodding at the children. "Don't worry, I'll keep them here."

The streets are not totally deserted, though there is a palpable sense of emptiness to them. The traffic is slow and unusually quiet. Everyone looks preoccupied, like automatons doing what they have to do, not knowing why. Our neighborhood militias are out in full force. They wear camouflage uniforms, with grenades jostling on their hips and Kalashnikovs slung on their shoulders. They watch the traffic sullenly and exchange mutually hostile looks with the noncombatants.

It is quiet at the college where I teach. The whole city is like a body sleeping fitfully after a nightmare, with a collective ear cocked for the inevitable sound of renewed fighting. The few students on campus are standing around, some listening to the radio, others recounting their latest experiences. These young people have come to maturity in the war and, like all of us, are at once accustomed to it and not. We should no longer be surprised by the violence, and yet we are, each time caught freshly in the trap.

"Do we have classes today?" a student asks me.

"I don't know. I suppose so. How many people are around?" Mutual shrugs. Mutual exchanges of that sad smile that we all understand. There is nothing more to be said.

To my office. A colleague is trying in vain to get a telephone line. We exchange weary greetings, not referring to the night before, simply making inquiries, always unanswered, about the best course of procedure. The secretary knocks at the door. "There is a department meeting at eleven," she announces.

The chair of the department goes by, the same tired smile

on her face. For some reason, we are all feeling sheepish, like naughty girls caught by each other doing something we shouldn't. "Don't forget to come at eleven. We have to discuss the freshman English program."

"You must be joking."

I know what she is going to say before she says it. "What can we do? We have to carry on."

On my way to class, I hear the expected sound again. I carry on. Entering the classroom, I am greeted not by the usual bustle of forty students but by that same smile on the ten or twelve faces in front of me. We shrug helplessly at each other and exchange a weary banter. "Where do you live?" "What is going on in your quarter?" "What horrors do you have to recount?" "What is the latest news?" Books remain unopened, but having been carefully stated by the administration at the last crisis, "Carry on" is the order of the day, so carry on we do. Descartes gets a quick going-over, his thought irrelevant and distant, the whole exercise adding to our sense of futility. No one in class is paying the slightest attention; my lecture is lifeless. I try desperately to concentrate my thoughts on rationality in seventeenth-century France as Beirut intrudes with yet another series of explosions. The class evaporates as students scramble half apologetically out of the room, mumbling about having to get home. We all try, politely but unsuccessfully, to disguise our relief at no longer having to struggle with Descartes.

I go to the faculty meeting. English language instruction is the main item on the agenda. We have gathered around the conference table, not quite believing that we are actually going to sit, in cold blood, and talk about English, as just a few miles away people are being shelled. But we do. A newcomer mumbles under his breath, "I don't believe this," but his comment just strengthens our resolve. We ignore his disbelief, repressing our own. "If we hadn't been doing this all these years, there wouldn't be a university today," someone says feebly, convincing no one by his argument.

The sound of the radio outside the conference room is tantalizing. Finally, a colleague leaves the room and returns a few minutes later. "Let's go home," he says quietly, grimly. "Such-and-such and so-and-so have happened. I'm sure no one will come to class this afternoon. I'm going home." He picks up his papers and, without further ado, leaves. We all scuttle away, trying to preserve a little dignity in the process but feeling foolish, cheated, indignant, imposed upon. We play no part in our own drama; we are playing a game with an unseen opponent who sets the rules and capriciously changes them, and who can therefore never be defeated. We haven't tried not playing at all.

After having stopped, inevitably, at the grocery store, where I nervously bandy cynically humorous remarks with the cashier, I reach home, collecting my children from my long-suffering neighbor on the way. I don't remember turning on the radio, but it is on as though through a will of its own, telling me, in a variety of presentations and slants, the most recent development in this crisis. Finally—in order to get a better grasp on things, a little in desperation to make sense out of the conflicting accounts offered by the partisan broadcasts— I turn to the official radio station. I say, "Once more," because I have tried dozens of times before, always to give up with impatience. Today is no exception.

The state radio is much given to euphemism. Unlike the others, it attempts neutrality and achieves only confusion: "The sound of guns can be heard," instead of, "So-and-so is fighting so-and-so." Almost invariably it speaks in the passive voice, giving syntax to the reality of its own impotence. The state is as powerless as the individual and goes through the same foolish, perfunctory motions of existence. I remember the moment in the early days of the war when the station, like the state for which it spoke, tried to pretend nothing was happening that it could not control. It was a fearful night. We were huddled, as usual, by the radio. Station after station around the world told the bitter news. The BBC, Voice of

America, Moscow, Monte Carlo—the whole world was head-lining Beirut and the deadly battles going on. When we turned to Beirut Radio, "La Comparasita" wafted out at our disbelieving ears. In the midst of our anxiety, we danced an impromptu tango, celebrating our own and our world's madness.

Years later, of course, it is not so funny, and I impatiently turn off the radio, sick to death of it anyway. As I am now thoroughly tired and nervous, incapable of any more useful activity, I start feverishly cleaning my house. The mindless, strenuous labor is therapeutic now; unable to bring any meaningful order to my life, I work desperately at creating order in my immediate surroundings. This is the only part of my universe over which I exercise any control, and so I wield my broom and my cloths, never pausing in my idiotic labor until I collapse. I light a cigarette and examine, distinterestedly but carefully, the calligraphy decorating a newly polished brass tray. Polished or not, it remains illegible, one curlicue meaninglessly linked to another. It is a mystery to me where each word begins and ends, let alone each phrase. The only word I have ever been able to make out, and that at moments of greater lucidity than this, is the *Allah* poised here and there, decipherable because of its separateness from the undecipherable tangle of the rest.

Ceasefires come and go; the battles rage on. Nothing is accomplished. The ends are mysterious anyway, so one doesn't know what they are meant to achieve. The rhythm of life is clear; visits to the shelter alternate with everyday life. Every morning the gunners take a break, and for a few hours people rush out to buy supplies, to check on their friends, to go to work. Between major clashes, a few days of total calm might reign.

And during that calm, life goes on, apparently meaninglessly, but in fact fraught with meaning in the midst of the surrounding violence. Embracing life instead of death, conviviality and solidarity instead of division and hatred, "carrying on" has come to mean not a blind and stupid clinging to a dead and buried past but a clear statement of a perceived future in which the hostilities of the war have no place. It is a serious act of resistance, and a dangerous one at that. Sometimes we do not understand this ourselves.

One night, the phone rings. "Aren't you coming? We're waiting for you. Have you forgotten that you are invited to dinner?"

"You're joking. First of all, I had forgotten about it. And if I had remembered I would have assumed you had canceled."

"Why should we cancel? Everyone's here. Come on: We're waiting for you."

"But—" "Come on; there is nothing tonight—*ma fi shi.*"

I confer hurriedly with my husband. At first we agree not to go. It is madness to go out, and who feels like a dinner party at a time like this, anyway? A few minutes later, we shrug at each other. Why not? We have to live, to grasp enjoyment when it comes.

The party is hilarious. After the tension of the last few days, a sense of abandon overcomes us. I am relieved that there is no political discussion of causes, effects, and apportionment of blame; none of that confidential exchange of highly significant gossip and anecdote; no prognoses; no quarrels between politically opposed partisans. I am sick of this talk. Everything changes around us but this never ends, going on and on, amid knots of bent heads and earnest faces. Only once does the subject of the war come up. A professor of political science whose opinion is taken seriously says, "It's all over. This ceasefire is going to hold." An explosion of machine guns and mortars answers his words even as he utters them. He raises his glass in a mock toast. "*Vive la guerre,*" he says, joining in the laughter, recognizing with the rest of us the futility of trying to make sense of what is happening.

As the evening progresses, so does the battle outside. We eat our dinner trying to keep our minds off the noise. At one point, one of the guests pauses, looks around at the apparent mindlessness of the proceedings, and then says quietly to me, "Someone should record this madness. Someone should write all of this down."

Finally, we can no longer ignore the situation as shells begin to fall nearby. We hastily take our leave and make our way home through the empty streets. By the time we get back, the battle is in full swing. We barely have time to collect the children and get to the shelter. For a short time, the glow of our evening's enjoyment strengthens us, but this soon fades as the gravity of the situation deepens.

The radio is on constantly, of course, and tuned from station to station, it provides the latest reports. Casualty lists are mounting. The battles have spread. The south is ablaze and so is the north, the mountains and the city. We are dazed as we listen to the names of villages and towns under attack. We have learned our local geography from these news accounts. The country is being pounded away. There will be nothing left, I think wearily, nothing. I am so tired, so very tired. At one point it used to seem to me that the very earth under our feet, writhing in the pain of the never-ending beating it was taking, would rise up in anger and shake us off as an abomination whose existence it could no longer tolerate. Today it seems to me that the earth itself has ceased even to want to protest its own abuse and suffers its agony dumbly, lying there passively, like a stupid beast, like me, like us all.

The shelling is concentrated on us now, as it will be for the next eleven hours. There is no military target nearby that we know of: Ours is a thoroughly residential area, and this bombardment is not the first outrage of this outrageous war. We sit, neighbors and families huddled together the whole night, fear giving way to disbelief and anger. What is going on? Who is bombing us? Why? As we collect ourselves for what seems to be inevitable death—for there is, at one point, no doubt in my mind at all that we are going to be buried under the rubble of our collapsing building—I feel more than ever that old anger. If I am going to die and my husband and children with me, I want to know who is killing me and why.

Strangely, I do not fear death. I have been too afraid of it too often and too long to take it as seriously as I once did. Its looming familiarity has rendered it less awesome, somehow less majestic, and I no longer feel like groveling at its feet. Years ago, when my eldest son was three or four, he once donned a particularly fearsome Halloween costume and, catching sight of himself in the mirror, collapsed into howls of terror. Trying to reassure and comfort him, I carried him, still howling and clutching me, to the mirror, where I demonstrated to him, by alternatively removing and returning the mask to his face, that it was only an image, a papier-mâché trick that had so frightened him. Gradually, his sobs subsided as he grew accustomed to the sight. Eventually gathering up his courage, he had turned to taunting the image in the mirror, running up to it to catch it by surprise and then running away again as soon as it looked at him. Howls of fear turned to howls of hysterical laughter, expressing not enjoyment so much as the necessity of testing the image and showing it up—even while still recognizing it as alien and persistently, doggedly, challenging.

That is rather how I feel about death now—my own death, that is. I do not look upon it, however, with such sanguinity when I think of the possible deaths of members of my family. I could not endure that cruel loss, I think.

I ponder, for the ten thousandth time since this damnable war began, on the happiness of the manufacturers and salesmen of arms and ammunition. Every roar, whistle, and crash translates itself in my mind to the sound of a cash register, the tinkle of champagne glasses, and the hum of conversation at a very expensive restaurant somewhere. The glisten of shrapnel, the smoke billowing out of someone's ruined home, the rumble of the big guns, are all echoed in my imagination as the glitter of jewelry, the smoke of cigars lazily puffed out of appreciative lips, and the rolling of drums for a hip-swinging, carefree dance. The screams of a terrified, burning child becomes the laughter of those who reap the gains of this havoc.

And the leaders, too—my anger and bitterness embraces them as well, from the leaders of the smallest, least significant local faction to the leaders of the great powers, regional and global, with their cynical maneuvering and ploys for power, their murderous games, their speeches and press conferences, their bulletproof limousines with silly little flags flying in the wind, this is their creation, this inferno is their great accomplishment.

Shell follows exploding shell. We can hear glass shattering and falling, concrete crumbling, and the tinkle of shrapnel landing. A red glow from the cars burning in the street outside casts an eerie shade on us, along with the erratic light from the gas lamp that someone has produced, which hisses away in a corner, now fading to a glimmer, now burning brightly.

Our war-long fear of the underground garage is now justified. A shell lands on the roof and part of the ceiling collapses. The rubble lands on one of the cars. For a few agonizing seconds we stare at it and then, relieved, relax. Luckily, the shell had exploded on impact. Had it not done so, we would have been—what? Burned? Asphyxiated? Could the force of the explosion have brought down the building over our heads? We were lucky this time. If another shell landed, would we escape again? No one dares do anything. It is impossible for anyone even to attempt to move out the cars. Shells are landing every few minutes. We are utterly helpless.

There is a flurry of excitement. "L has been hit," someone says. She had been sitting in a spot we now recognize as exposed, although it had served us in many past battles. She now sits in another place, covered with blood, a shrapnel wound in her head. Although there are two doctors with us, they are helpless. They have no disinfectant, no bandages. All our clothes are by now dirty and sooty. She simply sits there, holding compresses made of wads of tissues to her head, discarding them as they turn red through her fingers. It isn't until the next day that she will be able to go to the hospital and to have her wound cleaned and stitched. She is lucky. Tonight one man in the neighborhood, cut by flying glass, will bleed to death, right there as his family and friends watch, horrified.

Hours pass and gradually, with the dawn, quiet comes. The first order of business now is to take stock of the damage. The men go up one by one, carrying fire extinguishers, to check on the flats, each family praying that theirs was not hit. When the men return, relief on their faces, we learn that, miraculously, although our building has taken five or six direct hits, they are all on the central staircases or on balconies. But the shrapnel has done its work. There is hardly a pane of glass left intact; each home is a mess of twisted aluminum and shattered glass. Great coats of dust and soot cover everything. There are holes in the walls and ceilings where the shrapnel landed; shredded curtains blow in the wind; broken shutters and holes burned in the carpets create ugly patterns of light and dark, but nothing more serious has happened. It will take days to clean up—but we are all grateful.

Next we venture out to look at the neighborhood and to check on our friends and relatives. The sight takes our breath away. Eleven hours of direct artillery shelling on the area has left its mark. The street is lined with burned cars, all of them now the same shade of mustard yellow, some of them still smoking—one of them, indeed, still burning. Some of them lie upside down, some at crazy angles to one another. We remember the sound they had made as, one by one, they blew up; and the almost pleasant surprise the sound engendered in us as we sat that night: not a great roar, as you would have thought, but a gentle *pouf, pouf*—almost poetic, almost lyrical. The shops next door to us—or rather what is left of the shops, which isn't much—are still ablaze. The trees that had lined the street have been blown all over, their dismembered bodies strewn around, mingling with the glass and stones and burning cars, adding a strange, wintry look to the devastation. Electric wires and street lamps hang in disorderly lines and arcs, like a sloppy schoolboy's geometry exercise. Every building in sight stands gaping, shutters askew, glass hanging dangerously jagged from twisted aluminum frames, great and small holes everywhere. The atmosphere is thick with smoke and the smell of gasoline and fire. The streets are covered with a kind of ooze, not unlike the slushy combination of dirt and melting snow. But there is no snow, and I wonder, fascinated, as I tread in it, what this ooze is. It is as though the streets are bleeding.

A terrible hush lies over the ruins, and we whisper to each other in its weird presence, as we do in the presence of death. It is as though we humans who tread gingerly on the shattered streets are intruding on the mourning of these inanimate, broken things; as though we have stumbled unwanted into the privacy of their shamed disarray.

☐

The days pass. The glass is back in my windows, though it is dirty and still marked with the window maker's codes and the smudged finger marks left by his laborers. Through the dirty windows lined by my unmended torn curtains, I look out at the impassive sea. Outside, for the moment at least, the sound of building has replaced the sound of the guns: hammering, scraping, sweeping, cement pouring. The rubble has been swept into neat piles here and there, and every day some of the piles get carried away in beaten and battered trucks. The burned cars have disappeared. The buildings are being patched up.

It is not so easy to patch up the people. Some still sleep fully clothed. Some still refuse to leave their homes, sitting indoors, waiting. Some leap up, shaking, at the slightest sound. Eventually they will get on with things, although many of them will leave. Already there is a flurry of people packing up, as there is after each of these rounds of fighting.

A thousand miles away, a peace conference is being held. We do not know what the outcome will be but hope for the best, even as we prepare for the worst. I get ready to go to work. Classes resume today after weeks of disruption, and the children have already gone back to school. Nothing has changed.

A Glossary of Terms Used in Times of Crisis

As the war progressed, there grew up a new language which Beirutis on all sides adapted to life-saving use. Most of the words are perfectly ordinary, vernacular terms or refer to places that have achieved significance as landmarks in numerous battles, but subtle nuances have changed their meaning entirely. With a touch of irony here, a metaphorical use there, or even with their literal meaning intact but loaded with profound emotion, these words came to represent a body of experiences, memories, and hopes for the future.

Like an organic being, the vocabulary is in a constant state of growth and change. Words and meanings metamorphose endlessly. The following list can only hint at this extraordinary aspect of the war and provide a skeletal guide to those who wish to understand. In keeping with the tone and spirit of the words, only the most informal transliteration has been attempted in rendering them into English.

al'ane   It is being hooked or it is tangling
il'it   It has been hooked or it has tangled

This highly expressive pair of phrases indicate a confrontation between two or more parties (either individuals, or, more to the point, two or more militias, armies, parts of the same army or militia, or any other combination the reader cares to imagine) that have tangled in battle. They can also be used ironically as, for instance, *il'it* between two children or a husband and a wife. In Beirut, of course, irony and literalness are often indistinguishable, for the primary quality of irony, improbability, is one of the qualities of Beirut realities.

shu fi?	What's going on?
fi shi?	Anything wrong?
fi shi	Something
ma fi shi	Nothing

These apparently innocuous phrases are actually part of a life-saving code that Lebanese have developed in the face of sudden violence. You might be driving along in the bustle of the city, or on a scenic mountain road, and come to a traffic jam or a deserted stretch of road. Either of these could spell trouble. "*Shu fi? Fi shi?*" ("What's going on? Something?") you ask a passerby or a fellow driver. "*Ma fi shi*" ("Nothing"). "It's just a traffic jam or an empty road," he answers. Or else "*fi shi*" ("Something")—he has heard shouts or shots or, at any rate, something untoward—he is not quite sure what. The clinching "*Al'ane*" might come, and the responding question, "*Bain min wa min?*" ("Between whom and whom?") might lead to your identifying the elements involved. On the other hand it might not, and you could go home, having come within an inch of your life, none the wiser.

"*Ma fi shi*" may also be used ironically, as when all hell has broken loose but you say, "*Ma fi shi*," and smile bitterly.

tawattur	tension

A euphemism for incipient violence.

himyit	It is getting hot

The reference here is not to the weather but to the political climate.

khirbit al dinya	The world was destroyed
amit al iyameh	The day of judgment came

These are hyperbolic comments to indicate the intensity of the combat. In a country in which violence has become a way of life, people are often hard put to find words to describe the more awesome events. At one point, newspaper editors vied with each other to extricate from language headlines that could appropriately express each situation. In my view the longtime champion remained the French language daily *L'Orient-Le Jour* whose coverage encompassed levels beginning with the mild "*flambée*" to the middling "*paroxysme de violence*" to the superlative "*journée d'enfer*" and finally the crowning "*Cataclysme!*"

khaleena nrhouh nindub	Let us go and put ourselves away

Dub is the term used for putting away, for instance, sheets or towels or other inanimate objects in a drawer or closet. This phrase is a universally used expression of the noncombatants indicating that it is dangerous to be on the streets and best to be tucked away safely at home.

a'adna bil mamsha	We sat in the corridor
nzilna ala 'lmalja'	We went down to the shelter
ma tharakna	We didn't move

These phrases are a good barometer of the seriousness of the fight that the speaker has lived through. Corridors are sufficient shelter for machine-gun battles; the basement shelter is resorted to in extremis. Sometimes one doesn't budge because one judges that the battle outside is not serious or close enough, but sometimes one doesn't budge as a risky gesture of defiance, a foolhardy protest against the missiles. Not budging can also indicate fatalism, or a belief in the rules of the "ya nasseeb al watani" (see below).

haram, bi (bit) khaf iktir   Poor thing, he (she) is easily frightened.

One of the effects of a situation in which terrifying events are a daily occurrence—and in which there is nothing to do but endure them—is the deletion of courage and cowardice from moral character.

al ya naseeb al watani   the national lottery

There really is, even today, a national lottery that can win you millions of pounds. When used metaphorically, however, this phrase refers to the chances one takes going about one's business, for here in Beirut, everyday life is a gamble.

mashi-l hal   things are all right

This sad remark is usually made when the opposite is meant, and indicates that, in spite of everything, at least one is alive. Often said by someone whose house has been hit by a shell, or whose shop has been blown up, or whose car has been stolen, or who has otherwise suffered some material loss.

sihtak bil dinya   Your health is worth everything in the world

Most often, these words of condolence or cheer are offered to someone who has been robbed, whose house has been hit by a shell, whose shop has been blown up, whose car has been stolen, or who has otherwise suffered material loss.

la, haitha bab   No, that's a door

This expression is used when a loud sound is heard and everyone jumps—someone reassuringly says, "No, that's a door," as opposed to an explosion. The words may be used ironically as when a sound very clearly is an explosion and one still calls it *bab* ("door").

ibtihaj   jubilation

This reassuring expression indicates that a large volley of gunfire is not a battle, but a celebration of an event. The "event" could be a festival of some sort—for example, Easter, Christmas, the Prophet's Birthday, the Adha—or it could be a wedding (or a funeral), or someone's safe return from the pilgrimage to Mecca, or the triumph (or defeat) of a friendly (or enemy) power, such as the triumph of Ayatollah Khomeini or the demise of Anwar Sadat. *Ibtihaj* can also be used ironically.

am byitsalu   They are whiling away the time

This cynical remark is often made when, no particular crisis in progress, battle sounds are being heard.

tiyyarat   airplanes

Invariably, this word refers to the passage of Israeli planes over the city, a commonplace event generally announced by a couple of sonic booms followed by the thunder of anti-aircraft fire with a rattle of machine guns thrown in for good measure.

al aswa'   the souks, the downtown heart of Beirut

These words are often intended as reassurance. You might panic at hearing explosions, rockets, and machine guns, but someone will say, "Don't worry, it's only *al aswa'*." That is, "Don't worry, it's only downtown." Abandoned, destroyed, the *aswa'* serve now as a playing field for phantom guns and phantom gunners.

al mahawir at taqlidiya   the traditional lines of confrontation

The tradition referred to here is not the tradition of thousands of years of civilization, but the tradition of the last few years of war. The traditional fronts are those areas of the city that have acquired respectability as battle zones, as opposed to the parvenu zones that spring up unexpectedly anywhere.

khutut at tammas   lines of confrontation

This term almost invariably refers to the main dividing points between the two parts of the city, although it is sometimes used ironically to refer to divisions within either part of the city. The division is better known in English as the Green Line; although how that strange title came about no one that I know has ever been able to figure out, for there is nothing "green" at all about the line. Red, rather, with blood; or black, perhaps, with cruelty and pain—but not green.

al mathaf   the Museum

The National Museum was never a great cultural center. It contained a modest though attractive collection of antiquities gleaned from the long history of the country. Today, however, references to the museum no longer bear the slightest connotation of culture—except the culture of war—for the museum stands at the crossroads, right on the Green Line and presides, pockmarked and rather reduced in dignity, over the never-ending battles, and the endless stream of people crossing the line.

But the phrase *We took the Museum road* has, I think, another, hidden meaning. History, ancient and hoary, whose house is the museum, watches human folly in silence. Perhaps it, at least, understands our mysterious behavior and will pass the secret on to future generations just as it has passed on to us those equally mysterious treasures of a long-buried past.

Galerie Simaan   another of the confrontation spots and, therefore, crossing points.

Actually this is the name of a furniture store that has given its name to the area and which has thereby received more free advertising than any store in history. No doubt the owners of the shop would have been happier with less advertising, as this is one of the nastiest spots in Beirut and nothing of the shop remains but its name.

That immortality should thus come to a commercial establishment is quite fitting in this most commercial of warring cities.

Mar Mikhail   St. Michael

The church dedicated to St. Michael stands—or, to put it more accurately, stood, for it can hardly be said to stand when it has largely been reduced to rubble—just beyond Galerie Simaan and has marked for years one of the hottest battle spots in Lebanon. Along with the Museum, it deserves the crowning title when reference is made to *al mahawir at taqlidiya* (see above).

There is, I am told, an ancient tradition that the Archangel Michael's function was to receive the souls of the dead. What a supremely fitting site for a church dedicated to him!

Then, too, in the Book of Revelation, Michael presides over the war in heaven:

> *And there was war in heaven: Michael and his angels fought against the dragon; and the dragon fought and his angels.*
>
> *And prevailed not, neither was their place found any more in heaven.*
>
> *And the great dragon was cast out, that old serpent called the Devil, and Satan, which deceiveth the whole world: he was cast out into the earth, and his angels were cast out with him.*
>
> *—Revelation 7–9*

There is no need to search far from the church to find out where the Devil roams: If there was ever a spot on Earth where the darkest deeds were done, it is here. The warring groups perceive in their battles an apocalyptic confrontation, each side seeing the other as the very incarnation of evil and itself as the embodiment of good—each seeking to cast out the other forever.

musallaheen	Armed men
	elements armées (in French)

This term is used for members of a militia or army who are not on official business, for example, when they are conducting a robbery, or when someone suffering an encounter with them (say, in a traffic jam) is unable to identify the party to which they belong; for armed men all tend to behave in the same way towards the unarmed, and the unarmed tend to perceive them as equally threatening.

The term can also be used by political opponents when referring to members of each other's militias: If *X*'s soldiers are, in *Y*'s eyes *musallaheen*, they are in *X*'s eyes *abtal* ("heroes") or *munadileen* ("strugglers for the cause") and vice versa.

Then too, this elastic term can be used when, unwilling to point an incriminating finger where everyone knows in fact it should be pointed, one maintains neutrality in reporting an assassination, a kidnapping, or any other aggression.

qannas   sniper

This story circulated in Beirut: A veteran sniper, recruiting an acquaintance, was enthusiastically offering a job description. "You get paid," he concluded his pitch, "by the head. For each person you kill, you earn *X*." "But," wondered the prospective employee, "how do you prove how many you have killed?" "*Wallaw!*" answered the other indignantly. "They take your word for it. Is there no honor left in the world?"

istinfar   mobilization

As a porcupine, at the ready, bristles with pointed quills, so do the streets of Beirut bristle with armed men when an *istinfar* takes place. The men stand in uniform at streetcorners and at the barricades, guns poised. An *istinfar* is generally spontaneous, often arising from the men themselves, not from orders issued, and often follows a personal affront or another minor quarrel. Such confrontations can gradually fade away or—just as commonly—degenerate into an open battle. Wise civilians know that the best course of action is to prepare for the worst and scurry home as fast as possible.

istinfar moudad   countermobilization

If one group is in a state of *istinfar*, its enemies, feeling a threat and not to be outdone, respond in kind and collect themselves into an opposing *istinfar moudad*, perceiving themselves as the machinery that will shoot down the arrogant enemy.

khatf   kidnapping

A favorite pastime of the *musallaheen* is kidnapping. A kidnap victim may be a) killed, b) released unharmed, or c) exchanged for someone kidnapped on the other side. The victim, if released, will often issue a public statement of thanks to those who kidnapped him, praising them for their goodness, hospitality, and assistance—lest they try again.

anassir ghair bundabita   undisciplined elements

Each faction claims to be cursed with these elements, armed men who apparently do not obey ceasefire orders, and who are blamed for robberies, murders, bombings, and other forms of mayhem that occur squarely in their own territory but for which they offer only disclaimers. There is some suspicion, on the part of the noncombatant population, that these men do not exist at all, or at least, that they are merely a good excuse for useful activities that cannot be openly condoned.

One is reminded of the first Queen Elizabeth, publicly and in the presence of the Spanish ambassador to her court, scolding Drake and Frobisher for their piratical activities on the high seas and then, in the privacy of her chambers, congratulating them.

Were not the Sea Dogs the *anassir ghair bundabita* of Elizabethan England?

maktab   office

For some reason best known to themselves, the local militias have chosen to identify their indoor positions by this ordinary term, and it is used by everyone with no irony whatsoever.

The "office" site is unmistakable. Typically, from a

shabby upstairs window hangs a flag stamped with the militia's emblem, the window itself lined with sandbags. At the curb just outside the door, which is also lined with sandbags, is parked a jeep, minus license plates but sporting the party emblem. Tattered posters and death notices of assorted militiamen and leaders are glued to the walls one on top of the other, willy-nilly. On the sidewalk is a tattered chair. Sometimes reclining in it, but more often leaning against the wall, is one of the young men who function as resident guards. Inspiring little confidence, distinctly unshaven, he carries his gun or hides it behind the door, depending on circumstances. When circumstances require the visibility of the gun he wears a camouflage uniform. On more peaceful days, he wears blue jeans and a T-shirt. In and out of the building go more young men. Neighborhood residents react with consternation and dread when an "office" opens in their area, for, inevitably, "incidents" will occur among the *anassir ghair bundabita* (see above) of this group. Worse, the building becomes a potential target for bombs. Outdoors, the same position is called, of course *hajez* (see below).

hajez	road block or barricade

Here, the militiamen check papers and, if they approve of the passerby's identity, will wave him on. If not . . .

qasf ashwa'i	indiscriminate shelling
sayyara mufakhakha	booby-trapped car
ubwa nassifa	explosive device

Variations on the theme: violent death, maiming, and destruction. Composer: unknown. Performer: unknown. Audience: anyone who happens to be in the wrong place at the wrong time.

amneh wa salkeh   safe and smooth

In the early days of the war, an obscure newscaster by the extraordinary name of Sharif al Akhawi ("Noble and Brotherly!") achieved fame and the blessings of the noncombatant population by a regular radio bulletin on the conditions of roads in Beirut. Only if he proclaimed a road *amneh wa salkeh* would anyone venture to take it.

We did not notice when Noble and Brotherly faded out of our lives, gradually overwhelmed by the scale and breadth of the fighting. We heard rumors that he had had a nervous breakdown and then we heard that he had died of heart failure.

Could linguistic felicity ever have been better achieved than by this coincidence of name and function?

al-akhbar   the news

News broadcasts are the measure of a Lebanese day and are varied in their sources and reliability. The evening television news has become so familiar a part of everyone's life that intimacy reigns between the newscasters and their public. On a bad night, for instance, the newscaster might begin with a sad shrug and wistful smile, and a woebegone "What can I tell you?" On a good night, however, he might smile reassuringly at us. "Things look a little better today," he might start. At any rate, the degree of gravity or levity on his face on the screen is an instant signal of what is going on in Lebanon, and sometimes it is not even necessary to listen further to know how bad things are.

masdar mawthuk bihi   a source in which confidence can be placed

Given the divisions that plague the country and the fact that there are as many radio stations and newspapers as there are factions—and add to the mix the various foreign news agencies and broadcasts, newspapers, magazines—each event is inevitably announced and interpreted in myriad ways. Hence, it is natural that people seek some assurance of the reality of an event and the accuracy of its interpretation. There is nowhere to turn for certainty but to the anonymous *masdar mawthuk bihi*, who, in any case, is as elusive in the degree of his knowledge of things as he is in his identity. In other words, this source is merely another name for "Rumour, painted full of tongues."

badha nafas tawil	It needs a long breath
amalyyeh tawilleh	It is a long operation
amaliyyeh musharbakeh	It is a complex operation

These words are usually said with a sigh and a smile, after a lengthy discussion that starts out trying to clarify the latest crisis, but can only show the incredible complexity and hopelessness of things.

al mu'ammara	the Conspiracy
al mukhattat	the Plan

These are the real culprits behind our never-ending war. A novice in Lebanese politics might think there was only one Conspiracy or one Plan—and so there is, only this singularity differs from analysis to analysis. There is, for instance, the Israeli Conspiracy, the Palestinian Conspiracy, and the Syrian Conspiracy. There are Russian and American conspiracies. There are even conspiracies in which several of these conspiracies coincide, and others in which they clash.

The reader should not expect proponents of conspiracy theories to show alarm at their pervasiveness. Rather, a certain perverse comfort is taken from the assurance that someone, at least, knows what is going on and why.

mutafa'il	optimist
mutasha'im	pessimist
boomi	night owl, symbol of doom

Over the years, people here have obsessively posed the question to each other, "Are you optimistic or pessimistic?" This is a question of paramount importance, because on the answer ride future plans: whether to leave or to stay. "It's going to be all right," the optimist says, without having the least reason; while the pessimist, in equal ignorance, says gloomily, "It's very bad and it is going to get worse." Everyone would rather bump into an optimist on the streetcorner in casual conversation—for these terms tend to spring up precisely in this context—since he lifts one's spirits and gives one hope, even if one knows perfectly well that this is a passing moment and means nothing, and that the direction in which he points is merely pleasanter to contemplate than another. Conversely, the pessimist leaves one with a sinking feeling, for he only points out what is clearly visible anyway.

At all costs, however, one want to avoid the *boomi* who stands at the edge of the pessimist ranks, ready to fall into the abyss of despair and to drag down anyone who listens.

Many are the reputations lost (few are gained) on this gamble. One who has offered a glimpse into a happier future will, at the next and inevitable collapse of hope, be reprimanded by those who listened to him. One who has made gloomy predictions—there are more of those, and they have scored higher points in the game by far—is resented for his accuracy. As for the *boomi*, permanently stamped with realized gloom, he becomes a pariah because he symbolizes the very situation that he so graphically describes and which we would rather not recognize.

Better, if you live in Lebanon, to respond to the inevitable question of whether you are optimistic or pessimistic with a shrug and a vague smile, and avoid answering altogether.

waqf itlaq annar   ceasefire

May or may not mean a ceasefire.

hudu' nisbi   relative calm

It is in that insidious *relative*, of course, that the deathtrap lies. Relativity is established, one supposes, by numbers. Thus, if on a bad day three hundred people could be killed or wounded, then on a "relatively calm" one, only two or three might die. The reassuring phrase *hudu' nisbi* then will offer little comfort to the "relatively few" victims or their families.

ijtima'at mukathafa   intensive meetings
usually followed by
li mu'alajat alwad'   to improve, indeed, to cure, the situation

If all the people in Lebanon were told one day by a genie that they could have their secret wish fulfilled by the merest whiff of some magic smoke, I am sure that the vast majority would wish to be rendered invisible in order to sit in on one of those intensive, endless meetings to find out what on earth goes on that not only does not cure the situation but steadily makes it worse.

rah yiftah al matar   the airport is going to open
rah y salhu al kahraba   they are going to fix the electricity
mishi at telex   the telex is working
telefoni mishi   my phone is working

A friend once told me of a game called *salata* ("salad") that he and his siblings used to play as children in Damascus. The players sit in a circle and the first says: "I'd like to make a salad but I have no lettuce." The next says: "I'd like to make a salad but I have no lettuce or tomatoes." The next: "I'd like to make a salad but I have no lettuce, tomatoes, or garlic," and so on, each player having to reproduce the list in the right order and to add an item to it. This game, he said, is like living in Beirut. One day, the airport closes, the next the airport is still closed and the electricity goes, then the airport and the electricity still not in order, the telephone dies. . . .

Few take this humorous view of their quotidian suffering. The above phrases are usually uttered with a joy so profound and an emotion so deep as to be astonishing to those who have not shared in them.

thalath meemat	"the three Ms," namely
matar	airport
marfaq	port
ma'abir	crossing points

For months, the three Ms were the sticking point in negotiations, and it was said by the beleaguered population that only when the three of them were opened could there be peace. That was many years ago, however, and now the things that require opening are many more than three.

at ta'ifiyya	confessionalism
at ta'ayush at tai ifi	harmonious coexistence of the various faiths

Political power in Lebanon has been shared on a confessional basis, with each of the seventeen religious sects and ethnic groups represented in proportion to their weight in the total population. As the demographic proportions have changed the demand for a change in the power structure has grown. This has been one of the factors of the war. The largest share has been that of the Maronite Christians, closely followed by the Sunnite Muslims and then the Shiite Muslims: The Muslims, in general, and the Shiites, in particular, have been challenging the role of the Maronite supremacy in Lebanese politics, as have other Christian sects. Secularists of all denominations have opposed the system in its entirety. No official census has been taken since 1932, and thus the disputes of sectarian proportion has remained unsettled.

Publicly, all sides are against *at ta'ifiyya*, and celebrate *at ta'ayush at tai'ifi*. Who, then, is fighting a war?

muhajjar   refugee

If the war in Lebanon needed a symbol, the *muhajjar* would surely be it.

Actually, the proper translation of "refugee" is *laji'* with its parallel emphasis on "refuge or haven." *Muhajjar* has far more negative connotations, and the nuance is important. While the word *laji'* implies arrival and safety, the word *muhajjar* rests on departure and emigration; and in this particular grammatical form of enforced departure or emigration—the *muhajjar* is "one who is made to depart."

Of the hundreds of thousands of people who have been uprooted since this war began, no reference is ever made to them as *laji'in*, that word being reserved exclusively for the Palestinians who came to Lebanon for refuge, but even they, when they have been forced to move again, have become *muhajjareen* in the context of the war.

al hawadith   the events

This term refers to the war that began in 1975, unless otherwise specified: That is, people will sometimes refer to the "events" of 1958 or the "events" of 1973. Perhaps nothing expresses so well the poverty of language in conveying experience as this mild and faintly contemptuous understatement that, with its close relation to the Arabic word for "accident," summarizes a catastrophic national saga.

III

Beirut:
A New
Topography

BEIRUT is situated on the shores of the Mediterranean Sea, whose waters, blue most of the year in the temperate climate, become a foamy gray-green during the winter storms. They rush up then, roaring, at the rocks that lie under the Corniche, the palm-lined coastal road, and sometimes, when a storm is particularly ferocious, flood the wide avenue in certain spots. Most of the time, the water laps gently at the rocks. A little inland, the surrounding mountains are green where they are covered with trees, purple where only rocks dominate the landscape. In the winter they are capped white with snow. They rise directly behind the city, which is built on a promontory, and provide, with the sea, its dramatically beautiful setting.

Before the war, Beirut was an enormously important regional center of finance, commerce, learning, medicine, and social life. The cosmopolitanism of the city reflected the rollicking pluralism of its society, which was multisectarian and included many ethnic groups come to take refuge here from the vicissitudes of life elsewhere in the region. Beirut also enjoyed freedom of thought and speech, a free press, and a multiparty political system, all of which were its pride.

Although it is beautifully situated, Beirut was not in recent times a beautiful city in the classic sense. Like that of so many other commerical centers, its more modern architecture was of an uninspired mediocrity when it was not downright ugly. But the old buildings—the villas, the municipal structures, the law school, all with their great colonnaded arches, their louvered shutters, and their red-tiled roofs, their old gardens with cypress and cedars, oaks, and pines, with honeysuckle and jasmine, bougainvillea, and oleander—ah, the old buildings! One after another they fell prey to the war and now stand wounded, holes in the red roofs, shutters askew, balconies fallen, arched windows now without colored glass, like old women without teeth; the gardens brown and broken, the jasmine-covered walls broken, the trees broken, holes everywhere.

Even in the best of times, in the years before the war, Beirut was a chaotic place, its undisciplined traffic legendary. Its various quarters, each with its own character and function, were united by the downtown area at its heart, and all roads ultimately poured into that region. Here was the business center; the head offices of all the major banks, airlines, and businesses were located here. Here also were the specialized markets or *souks*: the gold market, the fish market, the tailors' market, the glass market, each one an ancient alley radiating away from the center, the palm-lined Place des Martyrs, or, as it was called, the Bourj.

Noisy and crowded, this square was wonderfully active,

and one felt the vitality of the city here. Buses and taxis met in the shade of the palms to take you anywhere you wanted to go in the country, north to Tripoli or south to Tyre, east to the mountains or west to the sea; the suntanned drivers stood by their vehicles, shirt sleeves rolled up, invitingly calling their destinations and the number of seats available. "Three places for Baalbeck," one would yell; "One for Bikfaya," another; "Two for Aley," "Three for Sidon," "One more for Jbeil." The names floated innocently on the air then; many of them are forbidden places now.

Winding away from the Bourj, the gold *souk* was lined with small shops, one right next to the other, the alley covered with a white canvas awning. In the shop windows hung, dazzling, hundreds of gold bracelets and bangles on lines, jingling as they turned when someone touched them; filigreed necklaces and earrings that caught the sun as they turned; yards and yards of gold chains; rings, cufflinks, coins—everything glittered and glistened in the hot sun, turning, and glistening some more. Sometimes, when it got very hot, the merchants would shade the gold by drawing white cotton curtains across the windows, but you could see the sparkle even through the cloth.

Churches and mosques stood side by side downtown. Islamic, Byzantine, and modern Western styles sometimes were identifiable in the same buildings, architectural evidence of the passage of time and history. The al-Omari mosque, an ancient structure, dominated the area in which it stood with its domes and arches. Not far away, the great Cappucin church with its gold paintings and domed ceilings was not an architectural splendor but was pleasing enough in its own way. How innocent the rivalries of those days seem now, as all these buildings are equally in ruins and inaccessible. The large building near the old Conservatoire Nationale de Musique that resembled an Ivy League chapel and in fact was the Protestant church is now reduced to a single wall standing in the midst of

rubble. Early on in the war, pianos and organs were systemati-
cally destroyed: There was a meaning to the destruction then,
and symbols counted for something. Later of course, the destruction was haphazard, and all-embracing.

Downtown, near the old House of Parliament, a small
square had been excavated in which, if you stood at street level
and looked down, you could see Roman columns and structures. Not far away, under the huge commercial building
called the Azarieh lay, we were told, the unexcavated ruins of
the Roman Law school, pride of Roman Berytus. Elsewhere
were Phoenician ruins. And other sites were being excavated
which made Roman and even Phoenician history seem like
yesterday. Neolithic remains have been uncovered under
Beirut, and the imagination floats here on a sea of time. At one
point during the war we heard a rumor that the downtown area
was deliberately not being allowed to return to normal, and
therefore the city was to remain divided because of the importance of the archaeological discoveries made when the buildings there were destroyed. Thus were the present and the
future to be sacrificed to the past, a poetic rumor indeed, and
more pleasing to contemplate than the harsher interpretations
which are more credible.

Souk al Tawila, or the long *souk*, was a narrow winding
street. On either side stood shops which sold clothes, underwear, material for knitting and embroidery, fabrics of all sorts,
domestic hardware—curtain rings, zippers, buttons, everything. At the end of the bustling alley another lay perpendicu-
lar to it, and here was Beirut's most famous restaurant, Ajame.
While newer places were more elegant, more cosmopolitan,
while French, Italian, Chinese food could be eaten elsewhere
off porcelain plates and with silver cutlery, here at Ajame was
the culinary heart of Beirut.

As you entered through the arched doors, you would pass
huge mounds of mangoes, custard apples, pomegranates,
grapes, figs, and whatever other fruit was in season. Once

settled after the long wait for a table, greeting acquaintances inevitably gathered here and the waiters, who year after year were the same, small, round, brown earthenware dishes would come to your table full of *foul, hummos* and *baba ghanouj,* pickles, olives, onions, salads of all sorts. You would cut a piece from the round loaves of warm bread served in small wicker baskets and dip into those dishes with the assurance that this was the best food of its kind in the world. Then would come your *shawarma, shish kabab,* fish, or other entrée, and then dessert, usually fresh fruit from that mound exhibited at the entrance, or ice cream made of that same fruit. Finally would come the coffee, bitter or sweet, served in small cups and lingered over. The restaurant was open all day and all night, and was invariably crowded.

The fish market was always smelly, dozens of species of fish were held up by the proud vendors, gleaming silver in the light, or lay in ice by the scales or sometimes even swam around in little tanks. In the vegetable market people yelled and shoved as they bought and sold and carried kilo after kilo of fruit and vegetables. In the *souk el franj,* or the foreigner's market, you could choose from an extraordinary variety of flowers, fruits, and vegetables: roses and camellias, mounds of mangoes and pineapples piled high; mushrooms and avocados and endives, lettuce and tomatoes, cucumbers and herbs, coconuts and everything else you could ever have desired. In the glass market, piles of colored plates lay on the sidewalks outside the shops, thousands of colored glasses and cups hung from hooks or teetered in stacks on the sidewalks by the plates. Everywhere was noise, bustle, action, smells, sounds, color, life.

Today, the *souks* are dead. Early on in the war, the downtown region was devastated, and the markets were all burnt down. The Bourj became the no-man's-land between the two halves of the city, and gradually weeds grew up and covered the spots where the bustle and life had been.

In the beginning, the lines of confrontation at the center shifted for months until they finally settled down to where they were to remain fixed, dividing the city between eastern and western portions, along the notorious Green Line, as it is called by foreigners, or, as Beirutis know it, *khutut at tammas*. This division in itself was the most traumatic of the many changes that the war produced in our environment.

The confrontation lines are marked by milestones of once-ordinary life—a museum, a harbor, a church, a shop, an oil company, a school—that have given their names to crossroads notorious in the context of the war. Here one crosses, sometimes at great peril, from one side of the now divided city to the other, from East Beirut to West Beirut, and vice versa. Other thoroughfares that, in another time when the idea did not exist that there were two sides to the city, are barricaded with mountains of sand, collapsed buildings, and a heart-stopping desolation, like the Bourj itself.

The crossing that is most often used is the one that goes by the National Museum. The museum building itself now serves only a military function, while dark rumors circulate as to the fate and whereabouts of the treasures that once lay within. Near the museum stand some Roman columns, reminders of the ancient history of the place, and under the columns lies the Tomb of the Unknown Soldier. Today, of course, the tomb is an ironic redundancy, as so many equally unknown but less-honored people have fallen here.

The avenue leading up to the museum is a wide one, lined with jacaranda trees that burst into blue-blossomed spendor in the summer. In the old days it was here that risers were erected on which dignitaries stood saluting as they viewed the annual National Day parade. On one side of the avenue is a race course, once swarming with horse lovers and gamblers. Today the occasional horse can be seen being walked through the rubble, horse and trainer shabby and slow, like their surroundings. On the other side of the road stand once-elegant but now ruined buildings, including some that were embassies. Here and there a tattered flag or a pockmarked national emblem hangs lopsided from a balcony where diplomats once hosted leisurely receptions and chatted and smoked over their drinks.

Prospective crossers present their papers first at one end of the avenue and then at the other, running the risk of being turned back at either end. In between is simply the long and humiliating walk, undertaken by thousands each day. Taxi drivers at either end offer rides away from the crossing, and occasionally an enterprising vendor sells fruit or pastries to beleaguered pedestrians. When the situation is bad, sniping or battles might erupt here, and over the years many have been caught on the road with nowhere to take cover before the passage is closed. People carry their bags and walk across the line in the rain or in the sweltering heat of summer while soldiers or militiamen watch, the indignity of the crossing worsened by the physical discomfort. When driving is permitted, the queue of cars is endless, and drivers often turn off their engines while their passengers get out and take a little stroll around the car, stopping to chat with a stranger who is sharing the long wait to be approved for crossing.

Not far from the museum crossing is one known as The Franciscaine, which takes its name, of course, from the Franciscan school whose colonnaded courtyards and scarred buildings mark the top of the path. This road is open only to pedestrian traffic, although an occasional military vehicle can be seen driving through. It is also different from the other crossing because it does not provide the full view that the military-minded require: snipers do not do well here. People make their way in sand or mud, following the path as it waves and wends through high grass. No one comes here without carrying a special pair of shoes with which to negotiate the rough ground. At one point, the Franciscaine crossing became famous for the *manakeesh bi zaatar* that some clever person had taken to selling here—the bread covered with thyme and oil still warm and particularly delicious and sought after following the long walk.

I have seen the most extraordinary sights here. Once I saw a bride standing in the sand in full wedding regalia, carrying a bouquet of roses and carnations and attended by a large family with many gaily decorated cars. At the other end of the passage and also in the sand, stood the bridegroom, similarly attended. They were waiting, I suppose, for the officiating priest or sheik—or, at any rate, for something, because neither group was making any move towards the other—but both groups were jovial and seemed boisterously expectant. As we passed everyone waved and smiled at them, wishing them well and offering congratulations. They smiled back and responded cheerfully and graciously to the well-wishers.

Another important road providing access from one part of the city to the other is the highway that leads past the port, or Beirut harbor, once a major regional center of shipping. This crossing is the most awesome because it is the one in which ruin is most visible. Here are totally gutted and collapsed buildings, buildings beyond repair, many of which were once beautiful, including several very old ones, with wonderful columns and arches, red-tiled roofs over sand-colored stone, pointed arched windows with stained glass to keep out the glare of the sun in gracious times when such things mattered. In the harbor across the street the hulls of half-sunken ships lie rusting in the water as seaweed drifts around, mixing with plastic bottles and old tin cans. Old fishing nets hang, torn and empty, from the skeletons of little boats rotting in the water. These haunting ruins surround one totally as one drives by and the sense of desolation is overpowering.

The barriers, once entirely artificial, have only partly achieved the intention of those who erected them. There now is a difference between East and West Beirut that never existed before. East Beirut has tended to be cleaner and more orderly, reflecting the greater degree of homogeneity of its people since the war. West Beirut has become more chaotic than ever but still boasts that pluralism that was once the principal pride of Beirutis and which, even here, is threatened. But the difference between one side and the other is staved off by those sullen people who stubbornly cross over, day after day by the thousands, some to go to work, others to visit friends and relatives, and many just to make a point.

We noticed these physical changes around us long before we noticed the changes within ourselves. We had to draw up a new map of our world, and we had no instruments to assist us except our wits and our senses. And our lives often depended on the accuracy of our construction, so it was a serious business, drawing up this map.

In addition to those downtown, buildings or whole streets that we once frequented were leveled. Some were reduced to a state of ghastly, lopsided ruin and decomposition, or, more often, marred by layers of scar tissue. Superb mountain forests in the background were transformed into charred wastelands. Sandy beaches became slums or concrete jungles, visual echoes of demographic flux. Refugees arriving in large numbers built hideous structures in the hurry necessitated by the urgency of their situation. The refugees have not all been poor, and the structures reflect the relative wealth of their owners. Luxurious apartment blocks can mutilate a landscape as much as—or perhaps more than—the low-lying bare concrete buildings of the poor, which have a less permanent air to them.

The streets of Beirut, even those that are relatively intact, provide a shifting landscape of memories and sorrow. Whenever I walk by one house, for instance, I remember with fresh pain my friend who lived in it and who was killed at a barricade one night years ago. At a streetcorner, I remember when the shell landed and killed the mother of my son's friend. By another house, I think of the family that was kidnapped and has not been heard of since, and by yet another, I remember the friend who left the country and never came back.

Each of these physical landmarks, and so many others like them, are milestones in my inner journey of pain. Memories wash over the map, and layers of time alter its shadings.

But there is another kind of change even more difficult to describe: In some places altered appearance is a function of an organic mutation, a kind of metamorphosis from one state of existence to another, from one meaning and function in the city's life to another, from one social, economic, or political symbol to another. In some cases, the changed meaning of a place is a direct reflection of the changed meaning of the country, and of the progress of the war. I live in the western part of the city, and, with the exception of the downtown area, it is this part that has seen the most change of this sort. No more dramatic example exists than in one of the major arteries of West Beirut, Hamra Street. Hamra is situated in that area called Ras Beirut, which is dominated by the American University of Beirut and many other centers of learning, and whose principal characteristic remains to this day a mixed population of coexisting faiths and the open mindedness that goes with that.

Before the war, many of the banks and businesses downtown opened important branches in the Hamra area. Some even moved their main offices there. In addition, cosmopolitan cafés, restaurants, and stylish cinemas, along with the most elegant boutiques in the city, made it the social center of Beirut for the middle classes and the wealthy. The proximity of the American University and the major newspaper offices made it also the center for the intelligentsia.

Fashion and style were important elements of antebellum Beirut—indeed, it could probably be safely argued that there was still, even during the war, more fashion and style here than in many other less violent places. The erosion of that fashionable veneer and the verve that went with it is sad not in itself so much as in the corresponding loss of a certain sense of humor, a cheerful insouciance in waving away more important things as irrelevant and insignificant. Somehow, style and fashion, with their emphasis on the passing and the new, had been a defense against that grim earnestness with which tyrannical ideologies had been embraced elsewhere in the modern world.

This lightness was symbolic, in a humorous sort of way, of something that Hamra exemplified: an almost boundless tolerance and freedom of thought. It was this that had made Hamra a center for the entire region. Its cafés had been meeting places for dissidents, intellectuals, and refugees. It was here that they could speak and listen, read and discuss each other's books, often published in Beirut even if banned in their own countries. Pressmen from everywhere filed their reports about large parts of Asia and Africa, as well as the Arab world, from their listening post here. Students and their teachers from the many Beirut universities sat for hours in animated and passionate discussion of national and regional issues. Beirut had been a window open to the world and everything in it, from the latest hemlines and colors, to the latest ideas. Now the window is in danger of closing, though it is not quite closed yet, not yet.

Indeed, antebellum Sharia al Hamra and the surrounding area was like a sacred temple to the elegant urban bourgeoisie, many of whom left the city altogether when the violence began to take its inexorable hold. The state and all its trappings, including the police and the army, were on the decline, challenged by the new power of the militias. As the war progressed, crowds from the suburban slums and refugee camps, as well as rural areas, moved to the city. Often these people's sons were the gun-wielders, and the visible signs of a social revolution were most obvious here. That the establishment had banished them from its consciousness, that they now affirmed their own presence, was reflected right here on the open streets of the city.

The newcomers had started to tread the holy ground gingerly and then, finding that there was in fact nothing to it, that the barriers had only been in their minds, had come in greater and greater numbers until the character of the place was ineradicably altered. The crowds that walk along the street today are composed mostly of young men in shirtsleeves ambling aimlessly along, as often as not in the middle of the street, heedless, except for an occasional exchange of good-humored curses with them, of the frustrated drivers in the never-ending traffic jam. Many of the young men are bearded and unkempt. At one point some wore the cowboy hats and boots that had mysteriously appeared in enormous quantities during the war, rapidly becoming a kind of uniform for these boys who had taken over Hamra during the fighting and made it their realm. They would patrol the street in their jeeps clutching their *dushkas*,* their bodies covered with an assortment of arms, from pistols in holsters, to daggers in sheaths, to hand grenades jostling on their hips, to the ubiquitous Kalashnikovs. Here and there, a T-shirt could be spotted, with *Penn State* emblazoned on it, or *Oxford University*, or with the strangely out-of-place grin of Snoopy, or Charlie Brown in one of his accustomed dilemmas.

The women in the crowd are a far cry from their predecessors. By and large, bourgeois cosmopolitanism has retreated dramatically. Where pedicured, well-shod women trod before, coarse-skinned, hard-working feet walk now. Here and there, a brilliant splash of color appears in the dress of a Kurdish woman, long white scarf flowing in the wind. Once I saw an old woman teetering along Hamra wearing a T-shirt that read *Keep Australia Clean*. An occasional former denizen of Hamra can be seen grimly picking her way through her abdicated territory, resentment and disgust firmly etched not only on her face, but in her posture and in the very manner in which she hurries down the street.

Piles of garbage dot the street. The municipal garbage truck seems, like Sisyphus, condemned to an eternally un-

---

*Mounted, recoilless rifles.

finished task. No sooner is one huge mound of refuse scooped up and piled onto the truck than another sprouts up in its place. Cigarette boxes, newspapers, sandwich wrappers, plastic bags patiently swept up by the street cleaners every morning—or at least those mornings when there are no battles—magically and instantly reappear. In spite of these constant efforts, one would think that Hamra had never been washed and, like a sick, scabby animal, is permanently scarred by its garbage.

Much of the downtown activities of the *souks* has been moved to Hamra. On the sidewalks in front of the elegant boutiques of yesteryear, many of which are closed or have changed hands—though some carry on a now-anachronistic trade—street vendors, once owners of small shops in the *souks*, lay their wares. Pajamas, pullovers, shirts, ties, aprons, nightgowns, leather jackets, umbrellas, shoes—all kinds of items lie on the sidewalks or on the backs of cars. Sometimes they are hung on wires slung between one lamppost and another. You can see people trying on clothing in the middle of the street as though they were in a private changing room, apparently heedless of the world around them.

Vendors push wooden carts down the street, hawking their wares. Here is a cart covered with green almonds; there, one sporting Ted Lapidus underwear. Here is one selling Sony radios; there, another with smuggled cigarettes. Here is a cart covered with watches, lighters, sunglasses, and keychains in dazzling array; there, another displaying every perfume known to France. Moving up and down the street, through and around the traffic, adding grandly to the noise and contributing to the traffic jam, is a series of cassette vendors pushing carts on which loudspeakers powered by car batteries achieve a kind of endless aural display. The deafening sounds of popular songs rendered by *derbake* (drum) and accordions, violins and crude singers, thunder out full blast from the rival vendors, each going his own way, each choosing his own music, and so creating a hideous kaleidoscope of noise.

Pandemonium reigns in the traffic. You can hear klaxons rendering "Au Claire de la Lune," "Yankee Doodle," "Happy Birthday," "La Marseillaise," or "God Save the King." Themes from the Fifth and Ninth Symphonies and dozens of other unlikely melodies blare out instead of, or rather together with, the more conventionally deafening beeps of the Fiats and Renaults not similarly equipped. And in the midst of these improbable sounds come the urgent wail of sirens attached to badly maimed and rusted little cars, full to the brim with young men having a whale of a time and looking as if each had set himself the challenge of breaking all existing records of outrageous driving. The final touches to this mechanized orchestration of automobile sounds are the roar of little cars, whose mufflers have sometimes been deliberately removed, shifting gears, followed by the inevitable screech of tires and the slamming on of brakes along with the deafening thunder of motorcycles zooming by at top speed. Intermingled with all this come staccato curses, calls, and laughter, like human piccolos adding embellishments to the march of time and change.

The many cafés of Hamra have changed from their prewar days. Although still patronized by journalists and intellectuals, they have lost some of their cosmopolitan nature. While espressos and cappuccinos are still served, in some of them *shawarma* has replaced chateaubriand as the pièce de résistance of the chef, and fast food the leisurely meals of long ago. The *mondaines* of Beirut no longer sit in these establishments, and men dominate by far their clientele.

If there were always beggars to be encountered on the street, today there is a far greater presence of a tragic human flotsam that no institution now functioning has the capacity to handle. The present visitor to Hamra unavoidably confronts deformities of the body that call up a paralyzing reaction in which compassion is lost to an overwhelming revulsion. There is the fat, elderly woman holding out one palm, with the other supporting what seems to be part of a protruding gut. There is the blind man whose age, if you can bear to look closely at him, you perceive couldn't be more than thirty, but who seems ancient. His voice, chanting *ayat* from the Koran, pierces all other sounds. He walks, or rather shuffles, down the street supported by a child of about ten, whose impassive countenance belies the horror of his life. The man seems to be losing control over his muscles: He jerks and starts and, every few paces, seems about to collapse but doesn't, and goes on jerking and starting and shuffling as the child steers him down the street, palm outstretched. In their wake comes a younger child, bent over double, who walks on all fours, and twists and turns as he makes his agonized progress down the street.

Skin diseases abound, and ulcerated limbs are exhibited on filthy mats. There is an assortment of truncated arms and legs, the tragedies of nature augmented by the work of the war. Bodies ending with hips make their way on a variety of devices: roller skates attached to the hips, or slippers on the hands, or various sorts of abbreviated wheelbarrows. In the midst of the vast crowd one is overwhelmed by the lonely agony of each of these desperate lives.

There are small children, barefoot and filthy, tagging along behind passers-by, clutching at them only to be shaken off like so many flies. There are palsied old men and women, sitting with their backs against marble walls, some with heads hung in senile sleep, some with faces upturned, wrinkled and dim-eyed, whimpering for money. Yet others sit with a mute look quite beyond despair, staring up at you as though with mild curiosity, wondering how you and they came to share this strange world.

Some of the blind beggars were as firm a fixture before the war as the white marble façade of Antoine's Bookshop. One of them, in particular, has become familiar, standing in front of Antoine's, cane extended in one hand, and in the other the small green sheets of the National Lottery, his eyes rimmed with a matching, unseeing green. I have often wondered whether he chose the bookshop for his post as a deliberately ironic gesture.

The mischievous, ubiquitous "Chiclets boys" of prewar days, darting around with little boxes of their wares and dirty bare feet, have largely disappeared, having graduated, one presumes, to plying guns instead of chewing gum. But the begging gypsy girls can still be seen, gold teeth flashing, absentmindedly chanting their tireless supplications: "God keep you," "God send you health," "God keep your children," "God send you success," "God send you a bride"—or a groom, or whatever their sharp eyes discern be your need— "God send you success in school." Then there were and are still the young mothers, with bare-bottomed toddlers either reluctantly dragged by their hands or lying insensible on the women's laps, drugged for convenience or desperately ill, depending on your perception and the extent of your sympathy.

And now, since the war, to all these have been added those whose minds are as crippled as the bodies of the others and who have chosen Hamra as their favorite haunt. There is a woman who can sometimes be seen lying flat on the sidewalk, stepped over by the passing crowds, or sometimes sitting on the curb, heedless of the cars that almost knock her off it, talking to herself at great length and with many gestures of defiance and anger. She wears a lopsided look: One of her eyes is wide open and the other shut, as though she were in a perpetual state of winking. Every now and then, a grin breaks the grime that covers her face to reveal an equally lopsided mouth, one side of it full of teeth and the other completely lacking. Her filthy gray hair gives her an appearance of age, but once, when I came face to face with her, I could see that she was probably quite young. She seems to survive only through the charity of the numerous food vendors in the area, from whose outstretched hands I have seen her receive a *falafel* sandwich, a Coke, or a slice of *shawarma* wrapped in a piece of bread.

There is the man with an enormous belly who sits, filthy and crosslegged, yogi-style, on the sidewalk, obsessively tearing strips of aluminum and placing them in small piles. There is the well-dressed man who sidles out of shadowy doorways to whisper obscenities in the ear of a passing victim who, recoiling in a panic, hurries desperately away. He then retreats back into the shadows until his next sally. There is another who seems always engaged in undressing on Hamra. Once, as he became aware of my glance, he looked up at me and I gasped at the murderous look in his eyes.

And if these people represent an extreme of human ruin, they have many companions in misery. They constitute a kind of hideous chorus, one chanting, one singing, one calling, one trying to sell worthless trifles, one begging, one silent. Helpless witness to all this agony, I had come to avoid the area, unwilling to see what I could do nothing about, too aware of the pain not to be freshly shocked each time I saw it.

On one of the rare occasions recently when I did walk on Hamra, I did so with a couple, old friends of ours who had been away for years and who had returned now to visit a dying parent. Preserved by their exile from the ravages of the war, they were fresh and fashionable still, and they expressed their horror and disbelief at what they saw as the demise of their own territory in such phrases as: "This is incredible! What has happened to Hamra! It was the Champs Elysées of Beirut, the Fifth Avenue, the Regent Street!"

I walked with them in growing sullenness, I think, and then reluctantly accepted their invitation to join them in taking a cup of coffee at one of the sidewalk cafés. To avoid the noise, we decided to sit inside rather than on the pavement. As we entered they saw a couple they had not seen for years and stood for a few minutes chatting with them. With some relief, I took out my still unread copy of that day's *L'Orient-Le Jour*. I glanced at the headline—*"Journée d'enfer au sud"*—and read of the latest horrors in the south. The account of yesterday's battle between two militias in West Beirut that had left many dead and wounded and which had started over a traffic accident was the second major story of the day. Having finished reading it, I glanced with some amusement at the advertisements, noting the sales at the Charles Jourdan and Yves St. Laurent boutiques, the forthcoming opening of the luxurious restaurant in East Beirut whose advent had been promised in extravagant terms for months, and the latest of the myriad new cinemas cropping up as well in East Beirut. I read of the latest robberies and holdups on both sides of the city and was turning to read *L'Orient*'s account of the latest fiasco in the attempt to form a new government when they returned and ordered the coffee.

Suddenly, gunfire exploded on the street outside, and dozens of people scurried into the café to take refuge from the battle. We discovered from one of the waiters who had interrogated a hysterical woman that two of the vendors, belonging to rival militias, had quarreled, zipped out their Kalashnikovs from under their wares, and were having an old-fashioned shootout on Hamra.

The street was suddenly deserted. Beirutis have broken all records for getting out of the way on time. It is incredible to see how quickly a street swarming with people can be transformed into ghostly emptiness. Shopkeepers close their doors and pull down their iron shutters, mothers scoop up their children and run, vendors scuttle away with their carts, and after an even more than usually furious beeping of horns, the traffic jam evaporates in no time at all.

As suddenly as the commotion started, it stopped, and as suddenly as Hamra was emptied, it filled up again; within a few minutes life went on as though nothing had happened.

Throughout this episode, my friends had sat in frozen expectation of catastrophe, and as it ended, they relaxed and watch me light another cigarette. "Don't you get nervous when these things happen?" he asked, as she eyed me curiously. "Of course I do. Can't you tell?" I tried to shake off the feeling that I was being examined for signs of mental derangement.

He leaned over and earnestly looking at me, he said, "Look, why don't you get out of here?" To my shaking head, he burst out impatiently, as she continued to stare. "There is no future here—can't you see that? This place is hopeless." He brightened. "Think of your children. Is this any place to raise a family? In the midst of all these gun battles, explosions, bombings, filth, chaos, anarchy?" He leaned over further, elbows pointing outward. "Do you remember that at the beginning of the war you said that one should either carry a gun or get out?" I did not, in fact, remember every having said such a thing, but I nodded cooperatively; it was the kind of easy thing we were all prone to saying at the beginning of the war when everything seemed clearer, and choices presented themselves in that kind of light. "Well, then, why are you still here?"

I sat uncommunicatively shaking my head, and he became visibly impatient and beckoned to the waiter. He settled the bill and said to his wife without further ceremony, "Let's go." We left the café together and parted after polite handshakes.

As I walked home, I was overcome by a momentary panic at the thought that he might have been right in his rebuke. Perhaps one reason those who have gone away have earned the resentment, however unreasonable and however much denied, of those who have stayed is that they always serve to remind us of lost opportunities of departure. They remind us that we may be making a fatal—literally, fatal—mistake in choosing to stay. But soon the unpleasant feeling receded, leaving only melancholy.

On my way home I stopped for comfort at a friend's house, but finding her out, I went as I so often do, into a small bookshop next door. The first time the neighborhood changed military hands after a battle, which it has done several times over the years, I had been alarmed and depressed by the fact that the store window had undergone a drastic change. The book jackets displayed there announced a new ideological content to the shop's supplies, one more in keeping with the new ruler's ideas. But on going inside and talking to the proprietor, who responded in careful whispers, I discovered that the contents were the same, only rearranged. The same books and magazines were there, only harder to find. Thus caution, brought about by imminent danger, had led to prudent hypocrisy, and freedom of thought was preserved. I was to note this phenomenon on numerous other occasions and at many other bookstores, and I was always relieved.

It was getting late and already dark, so I did not linger but started toward the alley near my house. The street lights were out in the alley, one or two of them shot to smithereens by bullets, the others victims of years of municipal neglect. The only lights available were that of the moon, shining down coldly on all our troubles, and of the small light of the flashlight I always carry. As I faced the alley, I stopped and hesitated for a long moment before embarking into it, so frighteningly empty did it appear. The mound of garbage seemed smaller than usual, and not even a single cat scrounged in it. The car repair shop outside which there was, in the daytime, always a bustle of activity surrounding bullet-ridden, windshield-shattered cars was closed, its workers gone home.

Covering the alley like a natural canopy are the branches of a massive oak. This magnificent tree is left over from the years, long ago, when Beirut was a garden city, clothed with cypresses, oaks, and banyans. Today there is scarcely a redeeming touch of green anywhere. Already this ill-fated tree is going the way of so much of the natural beauty here, through utility, carelessness, and stupidity. Hanging from a low branch is a wooden sign advertising a new shop; the middle branches are gradually falling victim to an assortment of electric, telephone, and even laundry lines; its trunk has inexplicably been painted a ghastly blue, matching the interior of a nearby grocery store. Passers-by asbentmindedly snap off bits of the lowest branches; trucks do worse damage as they crash against its side. One day, no doubt, it will be knocked over, chopped down, or otherwise destroyed, probably to make way for yet another ugly building.

That night even the tree was still. I started through the alley, carefully examining the latest graffiti in order to keep my mind off the possibility of a lurking thief or of a bomb hidden in the garbage. I read *The Shah is the Puppet of Imperialism, Revolution until Victory, Abu So-and-So's Forces passed here.* I read posters demanding the immediate restitution of the Imam Musa Sadr, who had disappeared years ago; announcements of the latest movies showing at the neighborhood theaters; dozens of death notices, including those stamped with militia insignias and pictures of their young heroes beaming out of their own obituaries.

As I moved down the street, I felt a swelling confidence—one might even say a strange kind of warmth—that grew, I must admit, as I neared the end. This awful, ugly, little street seemed in its abandoned desolation somehow no longer threatening but pitiful. I felt for it a kind of sympathy that astonished me, so accustomed was I here to feel only revulsion. The street had often reminded me of those poor, scarred bodies from which I had been turning helplessly away. But now in the moonlight—for I had very soon switched off my redundant little flashlight—it took on a pathetic and desolate beauty that has ever since lingered in my mind.

IV

Mirrors,
or Contradictions:
A Self-Portrait

I was born in Jerusalem, grew up in Cario, aged in America, and died in Beirut.

For years I have nursed this sentence in the hope that one day I would produce it at the beginning of a cultural autobiography that, using my life as a kind of microcosm, would illustrate some of the intractable conflicts that have exploded in the area. Although my life has been largely unrepresentative of the lives of the vast majority of people here, the very unrepresentativeness seems, oddly, to emphasize the nature of the body to which, however tangentially, I am attached. If Beirut, lying at the heart of things, has expressed the clash of social, religious, political, and cultural ideas, all of them foundering together in this chaos of violence—itself an idea—then

I find myself lying at the heart of Beirut, foundering in the foundering heart.

I was born in Jerusalem, which was then in Palestine. To have been born in Palestine means to be bound to a memory and to a sense of loss. The attempt to retrieve Palestine is at the center of the politics of the region; and to have Jerusalem stamped on one's passport is to be identified with this attempt and forever tied to it. A great part of the war in Lebanon has to do with the Palestinian question, and the presence of the PLO in Beirut was at least one of the factors that helped spark the conflict.

I grew up in Cairo, where I went to English schools and where my family, outsiders, belonged to a privileged class. In my early teens I experienced the Egyptian revolution, which was directed both against outsiders and the privileged. Although my sympathies were entirely on the side of the revolution, it played havoc with my life. In the war in Lebanon, class conflict also plays a major role, sometimes disguised, sometimes not; and there are many who would see the war also as part of an anti-imperialist movement of which the Egyptian revolution was an antecedent.

I aged in America. Here my opening sentence begins to become metaphorical. I went to America to college and almost immediately was wearied by the effort of trying to bridge a gulf between two worlds, the Arab and the Western. In the acutely uncomfortable position of having one foot firmly planted in each, I gradually came to feel like a kind of modern Atlas, holding up a mountain of hostility threatening to crush everything underneath it; or a female Janus, with one face looking this way and the other looking that. I felt that I had to reconcile the conflict, to explain one world to the other, but I had also to try to synthesize strains from both worlds warring within me. Both the inner and the outer conflicts began before I was aware of them—indeed, in the antiquity of collective and personal time—and continue to this day, as much in Lebanon as anywhere else, as does the aging and fatiguing process that they engender.

The crowning *died in Beirut* seems to me the best part of the sentence, and not only because it implies the living death that these last years of war have come to mean. As I do stand a good chance of dying in this dangerous city, metaphor modulates into possible literalness. The muddled past, present, and future become all tied up together. The *I* of my sentence widens here, from the particular to the general, as the danger of death confronts not only me, not only the thousands of others with whom I live and so many of their ideas, hopes, and ideals, but a whole society as well. The people of Beirut are struggling over a definition of what is dying here, and how much of it, and for how long. Does death mean extinction? Is resurrection possible? Or transmigration? Will there be judgment? Will a happier state ensue? eternal damnation?

Having arrived at these religious questions, I am less satisfied with my opening sentence, for it leaves out much that is complex and significant. Take, for instance, the problem of being a Christian living in a Muslim world in the age of what we thought was unbelief, but out of which have sprung theocracies and religious wars. I am not even an eastern Christian at that, not even with the benefit of centuries of incense and icons, magnificent, incomprehensible chants, and church bells ringing their dying peals on the mountain sunsets. I was raised in, of all unlikely, impossible, and cutoff ways, the Church of England, with

"The Lord be with   thy spii-riit,"
                       you." "And with
firmly squatting on the land that is my memory, while the natural and rightful inhabitants of my ancestral cultural heritage sit as refugee supplicants, visibly, perceptibly there, but held off by the barbed wire of the colonial experience.

And so, being a Protestant makes me not only a member of a minority but a minority among minorities. Still, it raises—

indeed, emphasizes—the question of minorities and majorities and what their clashes mean. Being a Protestant in Lebanon means being lumped, willy-nilly into that unfortunate category *Christian*, so totally and thoroughly misleading in the Lebanese context, so abused by so many of its adherents, so beloved of the international press and of all those who would simplify history. This conflict-within-a-conflict forces me to call the question of the meaning of the Christian life and heritage. And having been raised in the English church specifically calls to mind the realities of the imperial past, with all its vestiges, including, above all others, language, that priceless instrument of power.

Also lurking unexpressed in the *I* of my inspired opening sentence, is that part of me, simultaneously representative and not, which views the world through the universally bitter eye of womankind. Surveying the ruins that lie about me, and in which I had no hand, reflecting, with that cynicism reserved for the betrayed and the forgotten, on the demands for human rights made by all the factions here, another conflict rages. Modernity fights against tradition: The impulse to burn the bra struggles with the safer, easier recourse to the figurative veil. I know the modern tracts, but old traditions die hard, and ancient forms of duty and obedience do not vanish in a day. In any case, the veil today is no longer a figurative expression. Thousands of women are taking it up, voluntarily covering their faces and bodies, while many thousands more are watching them do so, horrified, and yet thousands more are fighting to tear it off their own faces.

There is more hidden meaning, in that *I*. I live and work in the context of the middle-class intelligentsia, which has set itself the task of articulating the wishes and hopes of the masses for whom it feels great sympathy. Yet, in point of fact, our life experiences and our training have alienated us from them: They have their own voice and often repudiate ours.

It is said that, as a person drowns, his whole life flashes

through his mind just before body and mind together are engulfed. Memory is the last gasp of life, then. Here in this sea of despair and waste and sadness that is Beirut, events call up moments that flash out of my past and interpret the present. I am led by them through a corridor of mirrors into which I have wandered, looking for understanding. Impelled by my own private agony as I flail against the overwhelming and pitiless force of things around me, I am brought up short sometimes by the reflection and sometimes by the reality. I cannot always tell which is which.

1

I was born in Jerusalem. My father was born in Jerusalem, and his parents before him. His father was a tour guide. A cherished family picture shows my grandfather mounted on a horse, while another shows my grandmother with a faint smile, and an even fainter squint, staring into the camera. My mother was born in Nazareth, where her father was a Baptist minister. Her mother, the only grandparent I knew, was from Lebanon, where her branch of the family still flourishes.

Long before I was born, my father had gone to Cairo to expand the business that he had founded with his cousin in Jerusalem. While we lived in Cairo, my parents used to take us to Jerusalem, which they considered home, every summer. Having crossed the desert by train, we used to stay in the family house, in which my widowed aunt, my father's sister, lived with her children, in the Talibiyah section of the city. This was in West Jerusalem, which was taken over by the Israelis after the war of 1948.

The year 1946 we spent entirely in Jerusalem. My brother went to St. George's School, where my father had gone, while my older sister and I were sent to the St Joseph's School for Girls. All I remember of the school is the play-ground, and nuns ringing the hand-held brass bell after playtime. They soon moved us to the Sisters of Zion school because my sister hated St. Joseph's and ran away from it repeatedly, terrified by one nun who had a habit of clacking castanets to achieve order in the playground. One of her playmates had told her that the nun held in her palm the bones of the naughty girls whom she had killed. My sister claims that she told me about this at the time, but I do not remember, nor, as far as I know, did I join in her rebellion as I would surely have done if I had been aware of this alarming rumor. My memory of the Sisters of Zion school also centers around the playground. I have an impression of a nun with a bristling mustache, but whether this phantom belonged to one school or the other I do not know.

Walking home from school with the other girls, satchel on my back, I used to pass the British soldiers sitting behind their sandbag barricades at streetcorners. I have a vague recollection of hearing about the blowing up of the King David Hotel, which I believe was not far away from where we lived, but otherwise my childhood memory of Jerusalem is a happy one, centered around the house and the family.

Our house was a large one, with a majestic staircase lined with potted plants leading up to an open porch on which much time was passed. I remember especially the garden, with long rows of tall marguerites—could they have been as tall as I remember them?—such tall marguerites, marguerites everywhere. I remember the smell of the house, the smell of olive oil and homemade soap, of good things to eat. I remember a constant bustle of women, including my mother and my aunt, around the entrance to the kitchen, always producing wonders from that inner sanctum, wiping their hands on towels tied to their waists as they cleared up afterwards. At Eastertime all the women would sit around a large table, making *ma'mul* and *ka'k*, and sometimes my sister and I would be asked to help by pressing the *ma'mul* dough into the wooden molds or pinching the designs in the dough of the *ka'k* with pincers specially made for the job. Making these exquisite pastries is tedious and delicate work, and I cannot imagine but that we must have been more of a nuisance than a help in it. Only recently did I discover that the Easter cakes have a symbolic meaning: The round *ma'mul*, full of crushed nuts and sugar and flavored with cinnamon and orange blossom water, represents the vinegar-soaked sponge offered to Christ on the cross; while the date-filled *ka'k* represents the crown of thorns. To me, however, *ma'mul* and *ka'k* will always represent community, and call up that picture of my mother and aunts making them at Eastertime in Jerusalem. My mother carried the tradition on to Cairo and then to Beirut; and no Easter has passed without the ritual making of *ma'mul* and *ka'k*. Although I have often assisted in their making, I have never done so alone and am not sure whether or not I will one day go to that trouble. If I do, it will be for only one reason—to keep alive this tie with the past.

We were in Cairo when the Palestine war broke out in 1948. A very dim picture of this time filters through the years: We would sit around the dining table, I in my usual place to my father's right, sitting on a cushion so I could reach the food. From that place he could easily send me, with a secret signal for which I was always ready, to fetch his cigarettes when my mother was least likely to notice. At the striking of the match and the first whiff of the odor, she would try as always to dissuade him from smoking and then, as always, give up after her brief plea was waved aside. Uncles, aunts, cousins, friends: There was always a parade of them there at the large table. They would come from Jerusalem, from Safad, from Haifa. I always knew when they came even before I saw them, from the extra places set and from the extra food. To me these visits used to mean that a little less notice taken of what I ate and how I ate it, a little less fuss was made over the necessity of consuming the last bite of vegetables as my parents performed their hospitable duty, casting their attention in a different direction, listening to stories, exchanging news with their guests, all of them laughing and happy to see each other again.

One time, although no one explained, it was clear even to

a small child that something awful had happened, and that it had happened far away. My aunt had come suddenly from Jerusalem, and she sat, small and round, occasionally shedding tears, wiping them away with the table napkin for which she had no better use, as she waved away the proferred dishes, unable to eat. Her grown sons sat and stood, stood and sat, ate and talked, gesticulating, pacing sometimes, their voices loud over her soft sniffles. No one was wearing black so I knew that there had been no death in the family, and I was far too young to know that the death of a country is mourned in a different way. No one paid the slightest attention to me and I was able, with great relief, to sneak away unnoticed from the dining table, taking refuge in my room from whatever it was that was so unpleasant.

The scene would be repeated over and over again, as the same uncles and aunts and cousins and friends who had visited before came now, all of them changed, all their faces drawn in the same way, all the discussions tense and nervous. I came to dread the visits that I had once enjoyed. In the old days there had always been little gifts and smiles, and now there was nothing but gloom and sadness. My father smoked more than ever, but now he no longer bothered to play out his little charade, and my special task at table was abolished. He brought the cigarettes with him openly and lit one after another, nor did my mother bother to scold him anymore for smoking too much.

I do not know whether some of the little details of that great watershed year and the loss of Palestine and of what that loss meant were gleaned from the conversations at those unhappy meals, or whether I placed them there—loose petals from a thousand dead flowers—as, year after year, the stories were retold: "All I got were the wedding pictures." "I wish I got the wedding pictures." "I didn't even have time to bring my jewelry." "We were working in the garden." "Just the clothes we were wearing, nothing else." "What about the shop?" "What about the olives?" "We were the last to leave. We were all alone. What could we do?" "I don't know what happened to him. The last time I saw him we were at my brother's house, and then I heard no more about him." "She went to her cousin's in Beirut." "The truck came for us at six. There was no time to pack anything."

Much later, 1948 assumed in my consciousness the grandness of history, of justice and politics, of natural destiny and international morality. In a little corner of my mind, however, history will always mean the tragic smashing of individual lives by its cruel hands and the scattering of bewildered people reeling from its blows.

Since 1948, of course, I have not seen West Jerusalem. I did, however, make several trips to East Jerusalem before 1967, when it too fell to the Israelis along with the West Bank. I spent the many hours exploring old Jerusalem, visiting the Dome of the Rock, the Aqsa mosque, the Church of the Holy Sepulchre. I have followed the Via Dolorosa through the narrow alleyways, and I have stood in the Garden of Gethsemane, my favorite spot in the city, admiring the view and feeling and—I am not embrarrassed to say it—the holiness of the place. Once I heard a service at the Russian church, with its magnificent choir of nuns.

The last time I was there was in 1966. My father was with me. He had not been to Jerusalem since 1948, having shunned it since its division, unwilling or unable to bear the pain of seeing it thus. He had only consented to come now because my cousin was getting married and had requested that he attend the wedding.

We went up to the top of the YMCA building near the Mandelbaum Gate, and he showed me with a hesitating finger, pointing across the barriers and the years, the streets of his childhood. His memory was dimmed by the passage of time, by the alterations of inexorable modernity, and by the tears that came as he saw again after so long the city that had once been alive to him with parents, brothers, cousins. Long-forgotten escapades of his childhood came back to him, stories of boyish pranks played on his long-suffering mother, whom he now credited with sainthood for having put up with them. He told me how he and his friends used to play tricks on unsuspecting pilgrims, misdirecting their pious footsteps when they asked for directions. An old man himself now, he felt a certain sympathy for his childhood victims, thinking how their legs must have ached, but still his eyes twinkled. I think that reliving of his childhood there at the top of the YMCA building, on the border of the divided city, his recounting it to me, was cathartic for him; and perhaps he came to terms of sorts with the loss and the barricades. But in passing his memories on to me, he passed also the burden of memory, central to the Palestinian experience.

2

In Cairo, we lived well in the midst of vast poverty. I was eleven when the revolution, led by Gamal Abdel Nasser, took place; and the convulsions that preceded the revolution in the form of riots and demonstrations used to close the schools for days on end. The revolution changed the pattern of society in Egypt, especially after the Suez War, and all the private, foreign-owned businesses were nationalized. My parents finally moved to Beirut in 1962.

I remember Cairo, the Cairo of my childhood, bathed in the dazzling summer sun; a white, shining city. On Saturdays, we would drive home to Zamalek through the hot streets, bustling with crowds of people and cars and bicycles, all of them shimmering in the haze of the desert heat. Policemen in white uniforms held whistles in their mouths, one white-gloved hand held up to stop this noisy flow of traffic, the other beckoning that flow on. I remember emerging on to the Corniche and Rue Maspero, past All Saints' Cathedral, that monument to British imperialism, since razed, and then on to the Bulak Bridge and to Gezira. The sun, brilliant and blinding, struck the hood of the car and the windshield, glanced off the windows of the great white buildings that lined the street, both on this bank of the Nile and on the other.

In the middle of this vision the Nile itself, the great river, shimmers and glides, long and silent, a great brilliant streak of quietness, through the centuries and into my heart and my memory.

I remember shopping expeditions in the grand car through the streets of prerevolutionary days; I tagged along into the shops behind my mother, whom all the saleswomen knew and greeted by name. She would knowingly feel materials, different qualities of silks and cottons and leathers, and I felt a kind of awe at the mystery of that knowledge and wondered if I should ever learn to tell a good cotton from one that wouldn't do. A quick trip would follow, perhaps, to Groppi, where cakes of architectural splendor sat majestically on silver platters. From great jars of chocolate and sweets my mother would select her weekly stock, which she would later lock up in a chest. At Easter we would go to Groppi to admire the chocolate rabbits and eggs, stunningly displayed, and at Christmas there was another pilgrimage to Groppi to look again at the sugar trees, gingerbread houses, and *bûches de Noël*.

Ours was a bustling household: five children, my parents, and my grandmother who often stayed with us. There were servants including, in those days before washing machines, the two washerwomen who would come in several times a week to deal with the copious laundry and the ironing man who would press the clothes, his heavy iron heated on charcoal. There was Lucy, the Armenian dressmaker who would come and stay for days at a time. Lucy and I were accomplices at mealtimes. She had a voracious appetite and used to sit next to me at lunch.

Under the tablecloth, I would stealthily pass her the things on my plate that I hated and that my mother insisted I eat—spinach, for instance, and okra and fish—and Lucy would consume those as well as the vast quantities of food that were piled onto her own plate. There was also Ninette, who would assist Lucy and who would come in regularly to help my mother with the mending.

My parents used to take us for evening drives along the banks of the Nile, my father relaxing at the wheel after a busy day at the office. He would drive us out of town somewhere, and we would stand for a long time, throwing pebbles into the silent water, watching the rings multiply and grow, while my brother would noisily break the quiet, trying to outdo his four sisters and get his pebbles to the other side of the river. Often we would drive out into the desert, where we would track down black beetles and trap them in jars, having punched holes for air in the lids. Later my mother would throw the jars away, the beetles still trapped inside.

My favorite excursions were to the Pyramids. Sometimes we would ride camels around them. I would climb onto the kneeling camel's back and then feel a thrill of fear when it rose, back legs first so that I felt I was going to fall off over its head, then the front legs, when I felt I was going to fall over backward. Then it would find its balance, and a sense of exhilaration would overcome me, as I sat at a splendid height above everything, swaying gently to the rhythm of the camel's gait. Sometimes we rode donkeys and, when we got older, horses. My parents would have tea at the Mena House Hotel, at the foot of the Pyramids, and we would run in the sand by the Sphinx or in the gardens of the Hotel, where they kept gazelles. We often went to the zoo, where we rode the elephant, threw breadcrumbs to the ducks in the pond, and watched the monkeys for hours at a time.

In the midst of these happy memories I become aware of a crack, a fault—an awareness I had even then that things were not as they should be. On those hot Saturdays I saw that there were two Cairos. There on the banks of the Nile, bound to it, and fixed by it, two visions blend, fade into each other, merge with the water, and then separate again into two distinct shapes. On the one side the great buildings, the cathedral, the offices, the shops, gleaming in the sun: my Cairo. On the other side, the black forms of the *milaya*-covered women, thousands of them milling about, suckling babies on large pale breasts carelessly pulled out from under the total blackness of their wraps. Suckling babies, the women mill about not only here in my memory of Cairo, their Cairo, but farther down the banks of time, laboring in the fields, with their men in white *galabiyas*—all stooped in the action of working that fertile earth of theirs.

I remember arriving home to quiet, tree-lined Zamalek, with its embassies guarded by policemen in white uniforms; polite dogs lifting their legs against dry trees, held on leashes by well-dressed women or their servants; children spilling out of the large car and racing into the cool darkness of the building in which we lived. The majestic Nubian *bouab* in his white robes and turban, standing aside like some gigantic phantom, held open the door of the lift. As we came racing in from the brilliant light outside, all we could see was this strangely large and powerful figure in white, the black face and hands disappearing as the result of the tricks the sun plays on the eyes. There was nothing servile in his servile gesture of holding the door: It is as though he were a picture composed of light and shadow, of white and black changing places with each other, one becoming the other, and then changing again, the real meaning of the picture now in the gesture, now in the power of that body and those robes.

Still, even in those heedless days—not, perhaps, so heedless after all—I wondered why he had to open the door for me; why even as we children raced into the lift, each of us anxious for the distinction of being the one to press the button, a sideways glance at that white figure caused a momentary discomfort that disappeared soon enough as we tumbled into the house with its comforts and the plentiful dining table. Perhaps it is from that moment and a thousand others like it that were born the feelings that we should, in some sort of reciprocation, hold the door open for him—for them—but blended with the ineffaceable memory of their holding the door open for us.

Always there was that crack in my contentment. One night in particular stands out in my memory. It was the first time I went to the opera. I went in holding my mother's hand, and I thought how grand she was in her beautiful dress and how grand the Opera House was with its red plush and gilt, its brilliant crystal lights. I saw the princess, the king's sister, stunningly beautiful, all eyes on her. She was wearing black velvet, cut low so that her skin seemed very white and shining; and her hair, parted in the middle, very black and shining. As she turned and talked to people to her right and left or lifted a graceful hand, the lights would catch the diamonds on her wrist and fingers and ears; they glittered so that I was almost faint with excitement. I don't remember what opera we saw that night, but I remember the applause, the excitement of being in this wonderful place with all those beautiful people, especially the princess. When we left, I saw her going down the stairs and getting into one of the red and black cars that were reserved for the royal family—no one else in Egypt was allowed to own a red car—and she rode away with a motocycle escort.

When we reached our own car, my mother held the door open for me to climb in—and then suddenly the magic ended as two children, barefoot and in rags, palms outstretched, came between me and my mother. It was from that moment, I think, that I came to see that mine was a dream world, a world of operas and fairy princesses, and that the real world—their world—was one of rags and shivers and the cruelty of a cold winter night.

Indeed, one January Saturday in 1952, the masses of Cairo rose up in fury and burned whole parts of the city to the ground. From the balcony in Zamalek where, on happier occasions, I dreamily used to follow the flight of falcons soaring high, high, up in the skies, and then suddenly diving, and the crows that noisily flapped around the public gardens near our house, we saw the red glow in the distance across the Nile. That Saturday, charred paper floated in the air, and my nostrils were black when I rubbed them. My father's business was among those burned, but he felt no rancor. He received the news stoically, with sadness. The next day he went to work to clean up after the rioters and the firemen. "I built it once," he said, "and I'll build it again."

In July of that year, the revolution took place. King Farouk was ushered out of Egypt with a twenty-one gun salute and to the sound of the royal national anthem that would never be heard again. After that they opened his palaces to the public, and we walked through the great rooms in which some of the personal belongings of the king and his entourage were displayed, wondering at the astonishing wealth of the royal family. Everyone emerged from those palaces shaking their heads, saying how unjust the whole system had been. We never saw the red and black cars again, but the full effect of the revolution was not felt until a few years later, after the Suez crisis.

In Cairo, I attended English schools. My last year in school coincided with the Suez War and the end of the British presence in Egypt. First I went to an English elementary school a block or two away from where we lived. In that vast cosmopolitan mixture that Cairo was in those days, children of all hues and cultures were tucked into the gray flannel tunics and berets, white shirts, and blue neckties, the uniform of the Gezira Preparatory School.

We would march into assembly every morning, divided

into houses named after Roman deities: Diana, Minerva, Aurora, Mars. We marched to military tunes pounded out on the piano by one of the schoolmistresses; "The British Grenadiers" was one of her favorites. Into the Assembly Hall then, and to morning prayers. This multinational, multireligious assortment of children would stand at attention and belt out "All Things Bright and Beautiful," or "All Glory, Laud, and Honor," and other supremely English hymns of praise to a Creator who presented himself to our minds in the guise of a bearded English gentleman of advanced years. Children of many religions, we all paid homage to the Church of England and heard the words of the Book of Common Prayer and the King James Bible, so that—private Arabic lessons at home notwithstanding—the English language was driven into our heads in all its glory and with nails of iron, day after day.

Like most of my friends and classmates, I was a Brownie, an apprentice in the scouting world. Brownie meetings in Cairo in the late 1940s and early 1950s were extraordinary: Revolution was brewing, Palestine was being destroyed, and I was going to Brownie meetings. The Brownies were divided into Elves, Sprites, Gnomes (I was a Sprite) and other figments of the English imagination. The Brown Owl—why an owl should lead a pack of fairies I never knew or, if I did, I have forgotten—would initiate the meetings for knot-tying, first aid, and other activities pronounced useful by Lord Baden-Powell, with a ceremonial *Tu whit, tu whit, tu whoo*, at which the chorus of childish voices would respond with an echoing *Tu whit, tu whit, tu whoo*. To this day the mysteries of that strange ceremony stand in my mind as symbolic of that even stranger unreality of which it was a part.

Every May Day the solemn Assembly Hall was converted into a make-believe green field. A maypole was erected in the middle of the room by the Egyptian *farashin*, or janitors, who were accustomed to the task but to whom it must have seemed, as I look back on it, the height of lunacy. There, holding blue, white, and pink ribbons, we whirled around the pole in intricate dances that we had to practice for weeks beforehand. Thus did we celebrate the coming of the English spring. By then, of course, the Egyptian summer would be well underway, which made the whole exercise as uncomfortable as it was anomalous.

At the GPS I was introduced to the English prefect system and to its chain of authority, beginning with class prefects, house prefects, and—the ultimate honor—school prefect. The prefects were children chosen by the school to keep order in the ranks, and their duties included meting out punishments to offenders who spoke when silence was required or who otherwise misbehaved in the playground or elsewhere. Punishment sometimes took the form of having to write lines renouncing the offense: "I will not speak in line," or "I will not push anyone," for instance. The number of lines depended on the severity of the prefect and on the gravity of the misdemeanor: twenty for a mild infringement, up to two hundred for a more serious one or one attended to by a particularly nasty prefect. A more terrible punishment was having to draw a map: "Do the Rhine valley," I remember being told on numerous occasions, "with thirty towns"; or, "Do Europe with all the borders and rivers." Boys' punishments included beatings, and tennis shoes were sometimes energetically applied to the offender's bottom.

There were ranks among the teachers as well, leading, of course, to the final authority of the headmistress. I remember one day this venerable lady coming into the classroom and saying gravely: "Children, stand up." This seems to have been a redundant order as we always used to leap to our feet when any teacher entered the classroom, let alone the headmistress. Still, I remember this particular "Children, stand up"; all of us looking at each other and wondering what mischief we had done to deserve her special attention. "Children, I have very sad news for us all. The King is dead. Long live the Queen." I think they dismissed us from school that day, and I am sure that it never entered our heads to suspect that she might be referring to the king of Egypt instead of the only king who counted, the king of England.

The English School, Cairo, to which one graduated after the GPS was more of the same. Senior school girl students wore gray skirts—the boys wore gray trousers—white blouses, ties and gray blazers. In the winter we wore berets, and in the summer straw hats. We were divided into competing houses, each with its symbol and necktie. Girls' houses were named after English duchies—Windsor, Kent, Gloucester, and York—while the boys' houses were named after those exemplary English heroes, Raleigh, Drake, Grenville, and Frobisher. We were taught hockey and netball and were trained not only in the fine art of playing cricket but in the even finer art of applauding it—it required polite clapping instead of the rousing cheers that were allowed for the track and field sports. We were taught good English morals—playing the game, keeping a stiff upper lip, and so on—and good English manners, sometimes with uproarious results such as occurred when we were required, against all custom and reason, to eat dates with knife and fork.

The school curriculum prepared us for the General Certificate of Education examinations, which came from England and were returned there for correction. As far as I know, the only concession to the fact that we were in Egypt was in the choice made by the school for the geography examination the year I took my GCE. Instead of being examined on the Rhine Valley, we were examined on the Nile Valley; both were offered by the examining board on a horizontal plane in which all places occupied a similar space in the consciousness. Living in Egypt, being part of it, was a secondary reality; real life was defined as centered on the British Isles.

I look back on those days long ago with fond amusement because, in spite of everything, the anachronistic education served us well. If it seems ridiculous that we were never taught

Egyptian or Arab history except from a European perspective and then only as footnotes to those chapters of our textbooks entitled "The Eastern Question," the close study of English history taught us a great deal: method, for one, analysis for another, and analogy for a third. And even if it were the "princely" virtues of the first Elizabeth that we studied, the qualities of our rulers were inevitably called into question. If we had to memorize at great length the intricate history of the English reform movements of the nineteenth century, the manifold and urgent reforms that society around us screamed for became clear.

We were not taught Arabic literature, the names of our great poets remaining for us at the time just names, but the study of English literature, taught as well and as thoroughly as it was, was not the less valuable. It made us, it is true, familiar with the skylarks and the nightingales, the daffodils and roses of England, leaving us strangers to the fauna and flora of Egypt. It made us think in terms of English rather than Egyptian seasons, putting us out of pace with our own climate. There was, for instance, a poem that we had to memorize. It had to do with November and presented that month as a gloomy, wet, most English experience. As it is, November is one of the loveliest months of the year in Cairo, and the fact that this very negative approach to it was totally contrary to the actual experience didn't seem, somehow, to matter very much. I don't know that I ever at the time noticed the conflict. It was as though we lived in two worlds simultaneously, neither encroaching on the reality of the other; or, to put it another way, each canceling out the other's reality, so that we were suspended in unreality altogether.

Still, the study of the Romantic poets extolling the beauties of the English countryside, which I had never seen, taught me to look at the yellow sands of Egypt, at the imposing cedar and pine-covered mountains of Lebanon, at the shimmering silver leaves of the olive trees, at the deep blue of the

Mediterranean fading into the lighter shade at the horizon.

In having to memorize the great speeches in *Hamlet* and *Macbeth*, I learned to think of the heights of humanity as well as its depths, to identify and to examine motives, and to hate tyranny and injustice in all their forms. I read Dickens and saw with sharper eyes the squalor and hypocrisy around me. I read Swift, and it was finally with the satirist's eye that I came to look at the world that had betrayed its own ideals.

In the meantime, other potentially contradictory sets enjoyed a happy if unequal coexistence in my life. If English was the language in which I felt more comfortable, the wealth, beauty, and diversity of Arabic always beckoned. My parents, and especially my mother, went to great pains to see to it that we learned Arabic, and later each of us would work further to achieve fluency in that splendid language, love of which grew over the years. If Arabic literature was not taught to us in school, its traditions and forms would later become sources of inspiration. The beauty of Arabic calligraphy presented itself first in my mother's expert penmanship, which was the model we followed as we learned to write, and later, of course, in the great works of Islamic art.

In this connection, I cannot help but remember with some amusement that from movies and books about Robin Hood and other sources, perhaps history studies at school, I learned of that man who in the West is called Saladin. Salaheddin al Ayyoubi was, of course, familiar to me as the archetypal hero of Arab history, the man who faced the Crusaders with the strength mixed with nobility that made us all proud. The great mosques and other monuments of Islamic history in Cairo and Jerusalem were, after all, part of my life and geography. It was some time before I became fully conscious that Saladin and Salaheddin were one and the same person, viewed from different perspectives on history. Similarly, I can never today use the word *crusade* except with a capital *C*, as it refers clearly to a historical event shorn of any pleasanter connotations.

At home, we took piano lessons and were instructed in the basic structures of Western music. We went to the opera and heard Puccini, Verdi, and even Gershwin performed by some of the great singers of the time. Arabic music, which we did not study, yet occupied a parallel, though less closely examined, space in our consciousness. It was, after all, all around us—on radios, on the streets. My mother occasionally used to accompany her brother, who was adept on the *oud*, ancestor of the lute, on her *derbake*, holding the instrument in her lap and drumming out the rhythmic modes for which she had an affinity.

My sisters and I studied ballet and had to participate in the obligatory end-of-the-year performances. We wore tutus and danced *en pointe* to the music of Tchaikovsky and Chopin. But I developed a great love of Arab forms of dance and thrilled to the folk rhythms of the sword dances, the *dabke*, and most of all, the virtuosity of such soloists as the great Tahiah Karioka, whom I once saw perform and whose brilliance I can never forget. I wince today at the so-called belly-dancers seen in Western movies, always remembering the artistry of Tahiah Karioka.

If we went to the opera regularly, we were also taken to the theater, where we absorbed the hilarious comic tradition of Egypt. In those days, American cinema dominated the screens of Cairo. Egyptian films then were relegated to the cheap theaters and were almost invariably advertised simply as "Arabic film," as though no title could redeem them from being homemade. Love of the Egyptian comic theater led me later to admire the Egyptian films and to complain, as I still do, that they are among the least-known and most-underestimated of the great cinematic traditions in the world.

We went to church every Sunday, yet the sound of the

athan from the minarets was as much part of my life as the sunset or the very air I breathed. I sometimes used to watch men praying on the street; sometimes I watched Ahmad, our *sufragi*, praying at home and was quiet, feeling his piety. During the holy month of Ramadan, I used to stand on the balcony at sunset and wait, as if I were a Muslim, for the sound of the gun booming in the distance to announce the end of the fast, over the silence of expectation that was almost palpably covering the city. So many of my friends were Muslims, so many of them were Jews, so many of them belonged to other Christian sects, that religious coexistence in those days was not a matter of theory, principle, or ideology. It was, quite simply, a way of life, and one that came so naturally to us that I became aware of it only when it was threatened later on.

We went to a variety of churches in Cairo: the American Presbyterian Church, St. Andrew's Church of Scotland, but most frequently and most influentially, All Saints Cathedral, the English church that represented the soul of the British presence in Egypt. It was at the cathedral that I went to Sunday school, received my catechism and was, at last, confirmed by the English Archbishop of the Middle East. At the cathedral, we imbibed ever and again the great rhythms and sonorities of the English language, perfectly delievered in full and majestic musicality by the English priests and bishops who presided at the services.

It was during the Suez crisis that an incident occurred that has long stood in my mind as the first time it was clear to me that relations between those various sets that had enjoyed such a cozy coexistence in my own life were skewed in the extreme. Although we never discussed politics at home or at school, it was impossible at the time of the Suez crisis not to. When the Suez Canal was nationalized, I was fifteen and it seemed to me, quite simply, an eminently fair action. When the combined British, French, and Israeli invasion of Egypt took place after the nationalization, I was indignant. With a naiveté born of absolute trust in those who had taught me fair play and the principles of justice that had evolved in that English society which was for so long the object of my studies, I assumed that the British, at least those who lived in Egypt, shared my indignation.

The Suez War began and the British who lived in Cairo were leaving the country. The English School was closed; it would soon reopen under Egyptian administration and with a new name, *Madrassat al Nasr* (Victory School). My friends and I went on a round of farewell visits to our old teachers. We were sad to see them go but did not really understand the gravity of the crisis. There were pictures of Gamal Abdel Nasser everywhere, and patriotic anthems blared from radios all over town. There were searchlights in the sky at night, and all our windows and car lights were blued. Air raid sirens sounded—although the battles were far away, there would be some forays on Cairo itself.

On that particular Sunday early on in the crisis, we were at St. Andrew's Church of Scotland. I sat between my friend and my sister, elbow touching elbow, stifled giggles producing an infection, an epidemic of shaking shoulders and strange grunts. Our heads were bowed in hypocritical piety and solemnity, and we clutched our stomachs lest they explode with laughter—aware, though we pretended not to be, of the chiding, sideways frowns of our parents, themselves caught in the dilemma of being outraged in church.

The Reverend S. stood at the pulpit. In his thick Scottish accent, he thundered, as much as his slight frame would permit thundering, the ancient words from *Exodus* recounting the defeat of Pharaoh's army.

Whether or not he did, in fact, wave his clenched fists as, armed with the resonant authority of the Old Testament, he delivered his sermon on the text, that is how I remember him. I believe he saw himself as the personification of a slighted but avenging British empire, with the Lord on his side.

"And the Lorrrrd *SMOT* the Egyptians," he bellowed. Part of the comedy of the moment lay in the knowledge that this unaccustomed bellicosity was coming from an unusually timid and softspoken man, painfully shy and stammeringly hesitant on other occasions. He stood in front of us now, transfigured by his sense of righteous anger, his sense that his was the book, and his language that gave him the authority to say, "And the Lorrrrd *SMOT* the Egyptians."

Our outrage was lessened by the comedy and by the newness of the experience; our sense of the ridiculous overshadowed our sense of the wrong done in the name of righteousness and divine authority. The comedy took the malignant edge off the words. The sense that a whole culture could be turned loose, like a gigantic serpent, to bite us at random was new to us, if not to our parents; but now we were protected by our childishness, and laughter was our great sword.

Later, the serpent was not so easily destroyed.

3

After finishing the school year, at Madrassat al Nasr, which included a brief representation of modern history—especially an account of British imperialism—I went to the United States and to college.

Before college my only trip to America had taken place when I was seven and was sent to a summer camp in Maine. I remember with great pleasure the summer camp traditions: rowing and swimming in the lake, nature walks and campfires, log cabins and outhouses, mosquitoes and poison ivy (I later tried, with no success, to create the same enthusiasm for these in my children), but hardly anything else about the country from that trip.

From my earliest awareness of it, America had been presented to me partly through the veil of its traditional mythology: land of opportunity, freedom, equality, and justice for all; land of plenty. Much of this idealization was transmitted by my father, who had gone to the United States as a very young man and spent years there before returning to the Middle East. Every Thanksgiving we were taken to the American Church in Cairo, where we learned to sing "God of our Fathers" and then had turkey and sweet potatoes for lunch. On the Fourth of July, we went to the picnics at the American Embassy, where we ate hot dogs and Crackerjacks and watched the square dancing.

From Hollywood I got the impression that Americans were all beautiful people, many of whom sang beautiful songs and lived in beautiful houses. On one of my birthdays after I learned to read, I was given a collection of short biographies of great men, which must have been an American edition because all the great men in it were of that nationality. It was one of those sentimental volumes deemed fit for a girl of my age, with many happy pictures: Lincoln, of course, was standing in front of the inevitable log cabin; and Bell and Edison struck poses of wonderment in front of their inventions. Washington rode a horse—he was looking backward at something that interested him but which I could not see though I tried very hard. Jefferson and Franklin were, no doubt, signing the Declaration of Independence; although the precise nature of this document eluded me, I was sure it was very noble and had something to do with freedom.

As a result of all this, I thought of Americans as those who had fought against slavery, not as those who had owned slaves. Of the Native Americans and their tragic history, I knew nothing at all except, again, what Hollywood had taught me—that they were a ferociously savage and half-naked lot, nightmarishly painted over, sporting funny feather hats; speaking, when they spoke at all, a very peculiar form of English; descending most unreasonably and with bloodthirsty yells, brandishing axes, on the defenseless women and brave men of the movies; burning everything in sight and then disappearing, still yelling, leaving behind smoking ruins and dead bodies, often with a small child sobbing over one of them. It was later that I came to have immense sympathy for the Native Americans, not only for the immeasurable loss they had suffered and for their reduction from a proud and free people to their present state, but also to the manner in which they were stripped, in these standard depictions, of even the redeeming dignity of that loss.

In school, America had scarcely been mentioned and when it was, for instance, in Geography, the names of its cities and states were almost invariably mispronounced: *Tchicago*, or *Coloraydo* or *MissISSipi*, as though it were a Latin word. I remember one of my teachers taking great delight in mocking the quaint American notion that a word written *Arkansas* should be pronounced *Arkansaw*, especially as there was a similar word—*Kansas*—that had not suffered the same phonetically illogical fate. (Looking back on it, I am surprised that we didn't turn the tables on this teacher and berate him for some of the mysterious pronunciations of English place names. New students were always surprised by the chuckles that arose the instant their unpracticed lips gave sound to that redundant *w* in *Warwick* or that mischievous extra syllable in *Gloucester*. Perhaps we did protest, and I have forgotten, or perhaps we assumed that English logic was, in an absolute way, and particularly in the realm of language, irreproachable).

In History, America came under the chapters devoted to the Renaissance, and Christopher Columbus was generally offered up as a member of the opposition who had delivered the prize, such as it was, to the Catholics; the true heroes being, of course, Drake, Raleigh, and their colleagues in piracy. In this context I remember that John Masefield's poem "Cargoes" was given us for obligatory memorization at least in part for its description of the "stately Spanish galleons" against which the sea dogs had pitted their marine wits and their small English ships and won, hands down!

Most of our teachers had colonial backgrounds, having taught in the African and Asian properties of Britain before coming to Egypt. Mombasa, not New York, Nairobi and Delhi, not Boston and San Francisco—these were the familiar places of reference. When the American Revolution was studied, it was from King George's viewpoint, a paragraph or two as prologue to that greater event, the French Revolution; and even that was seen through English eyes—Burke's and Dickens', for instance.

So, when I finally did get to America, I was totally unprepared for its reality. It was the late 1950s, and I was going to college. I will not dwell on the familiar shocks that America presented; principally, I suppose, I was astonished at the enormous size of everything: streets, buildings, cars, ice cream cones, the people themselves. I felt a little like Gulliver in Brobdingnag, but then so does everyone, I think, going there for the first time. Nor will I dwell on the more personal shocks I experienced, as a young woman come from the bosom of an extremely conservative society and plunged into the company of girls raised, by and large, in New York and its environs. I remember the first time I saw a girl my age take out a cigarette and light it; I believe I almost fainted. She did it not furtively, not with a glance over her shoulder, or with daring defiance, but quite matter-of-factly, as though it were the most natural thing in the world. And then, one time my newfound friends suggested that we "go out" and I found myself in a bar. While they drank beer I sat in total mortification, my untouched stein in front of me, feeling as though I had compromised my honor forever. And then again, I came to understand the kind of relations these young women had with men—unthinkable to me at the time.

Still, all these things could have been borne by the shock

absorbers of custom and social attitudes bred into me: The tradition of generations could have withstood the onslaught. It was the readings that ineradicably altered the way I looked at things, both at home and abroad, and penetrated not only the world I had come to live in but the one I had left. With new eyes, I reexamined everything and found myself simultaneously familiar with and alien to both cultures.

America was in the process of demythologizing itself, spurred on in this task by the civil rights movement, which was then beginning to flower: Little Rock was the news at the time. The Freshman English course to which I was assigned was designed, I am sure as I look back on it, to jolt middle-class American girls out of their complacency; and I was carried along by the wave. Once you learn to look at one myth and see it for what it is, it is next to impossible ever again to revere any other.

Reading H. L. Mencken (and for the occasion, being introduced to the word *iconoclast*) was an intellectual exercise not as shocking to me as it was to many of my classmates, his subjects being often so purely American that I was unfamiliar with them. It was the manner he used in smashing American icons that counted for me; and, sitting here in Beirut decades later, I feel the real lack in the intellectual environment of anything like his humorous brutality, for there are not a few icons that greatly deserve smashing here.

Reading James Baldwin forced me to think not only of the specific injustices that black Americans suffered and of their demand for restitution, but of the sad fate of all those trapped in any society by their differences with a hostile majority. Reading e.e. cummings' poetry, and George Orwell's essay "Politics and the English Language," not to mention *1984*, made me understand the vast importance of language and its instruction as an unseen instrument of immense power, and as a definition of orthodoxy and its acceptance.

Bertrand Russell's "Why I Am Not a Christian" and other

essays, Freud's *Introductory Lectures on Psycho-Analysis*, and Ibsen's plays, particularly *A Doll's House* and *Ghosts*, together with the companion volume, Shaw's *Quintessence of Ibsenism*, were, I remember, the battering rams that finally brought the intellectual and moral gates crashing down about me. Never again could I accept unquestioningly the givens of the society in which I had been raised. Stone by stone, the house I had been brought up in was torn down.

It was then easier to accept and admire those aspects of America that would otherwise have remained only alien mysteries—the struggle towards egalitarianism; the practical efficiency of everyday, do-it-yourself life, unfettered by social niceties; the courage of individuals pursuing, often at great cost, their ideals and desires; the secularism that protected individual belief; the openness of personal relationships; the notion, however imperfectly applied, of equal justice before the law; the pervasive rationalism and pragmatism; the looking, always the looking toward the future, like the astronauts who had just begun their journeys and who symbolized this view, with its infinite possibilities both of horror and hope, rather than toward an oppressive and ever-present past.

And yet it was only a part of me that was won over and, prepared by my childhood education, remains forever in the thrall of the Western cultural system, alienated from the traditions and values of my ancestry. The other part of me is as thoroughly alienated from the adopted culture and loyally clings, with a tenacity strengthened by experience and the failure of communications, to the very people from whom I had been separated and to their values and history.

The exhilaration of finding myself in a new world was dampened not only by natural nostalgia for the warmth of home. I found myself, as the years passed and my circle of acquaintance and experience grew, warmed by many personal friendships and kindnesses, but always coming up against an intruding and poisonous rancor. For there was, I found, instilled into the American imagination an image of the Arab world that was, to say the least, hostile. It was an image of barbarism and cruelty, of strangeness and inhumanity, of evil machinations and idolatry; of mendacity, mendicancy, and greed. I would bump into this image, startled by its viciousness, time and again, in television shows and movies, in crossword puzzles and comic strips, in novels and plays; and each time I felt the wound afresh.

It was against this image that I had to measure my own reality. It became an essential part of my life to defend myself—for the attack was so much of a broadside that it had to include me and all those I knew—and in doing so, I had to scrutinize my very existence. Finally, part of me became fixed in a pulgilistic stance that could never be allowed to relax, lest the self-declared opponent strike a killing blow.

To that which was so abused and denied, I became more firmly attached. In having to defend a whole culture against inexact accusation, I had to articulate my thoughts on it and therefore to know it better than I would have done without such provocation; to sift out the better qualities from the worse and to view those with deepening affection. Thus I became a hostage to a past from which I might have been freed, that I might have shed as naturally as a snake its old skin, had I—and it—been left in peace. Under attack, we were shackled together, the past and I.

I remain to this day a divided mind and soul, the two parts of me locked in each other's arms, now in warm embrace, now wrestling with each other in hopeless struggle, vying with each other for ascendancy. The parts remain equal in strength; and if at any given moment the one rises triumphant, the other inevitably pulls it down again, and the combat is resumed. They are mirror opposites of each other, each reflecting the other's reality, but each showing up the other as unreal, incomplete, distorted. I do not know whether it will be possible for them ever to relax into a more productive synthesis, but I know that were it possible I should be at peace and would have a better, richer future.

A turning point in my consciousness took place when I was invited—I believe it was at the end of my freshman or at the beginning of my sophomore year—to join in a panel discussion on the place of women in the Arab world. I knew next to nothing about the subject except what I had myself experienced: I had no statistics, no serious knowledge of Islamic precepts on the subject, no sense whatever of the consequences of the rivalry between professional and domestic duties and its impact on tradition. I was merely a young woman who had left home and had been thrust into a new world, who had come to recognize the differences between the way I had been raised and the way my new friends had been. I had come to accept their way, after I had recovered from my shock, as natural to them and was eager to entertain them with anecdotes of my own life that I thought would amuse them and make them understand, simply, that there was another way, another world, another view of things of which they were oblivious. I had been away long enough to see that there was much that was strange—funny, even—in the way I had been brought up. My preparation for the panel, then, was exclusively to think on the differences between my life and theirs and to marshal some memories with which to regale them.

Principally I was going to tell them about how sheltered my life had been from men and sexuality; how I had never "dated" and how that practice would have been regarded with abhorrence by my parents; how one of my school chums had been forced into an early marriage by her parents and how she had come to school one day, transformed from a uniformed schoolgirl into a married woman with high heels and jewelry, and had warned us all, as we gathered around her, awed, never under any circumstance to marry, describing with fresh disgust every detail of her wedding night as we listened in amazed sympathy. To me, the most striking difference between our lives was that my new friends had an easy way with men, that they could talk and laugh with them without the slightest compunction; while I, victim of a puritannical alliance between Protestantism and Islam, had been reduced to blushing and stammering paralysis at those freshman mixers to which I had gone so thoroughly unprepared.

My eagerness soon faded. The audience, which seemed much too large for the stated objective of the discussion and in which my friends' comforting faces were sprinkled among many I had never seen before, was impatient with the topic; and, opening statements of the discussants formally made and over with, launched an attack which almost literally took my breath away.

"Why do you hate Jews?" "Why do you want to throw all the Jews into the sea?" "Why can't one hundred million Arabs leave two million Jews in peace?" "Haven't they suffered enough for your liking?" "Why should you deprive Jews of their right to their ancestral land?"

They brandished clippings from the *New York Times*; they quoted, or claimed to quote, from a hundred books and articles by people whose names I had never heard; they twisted statements made by Gamal Abdel Nasser and thrust them, smelly objects now, at my face; they took the history that I had lived and which I knew from the living of it only, turned it upside down and trampled on it. I had no weapon with which to fight except my lived knowledge: 1956 was fresh in my mind, and even in my apolitical view of things, the nationalization of the Suez Canal had seemed the essence of a historically justified action and the subsequent invasion of Egypt by the British, French, and Israelis unwarranted by any standard of morality. In my naïveté I had assumed that all Americans who believed in freedom would share this clear view. After all, it had been American power that had put an end to the joint invasion.

As for the whole question of Palestine and the Jews, I

knew that while Jews had been victims in Europe, they certainly were not in Palestine: The broken lives of all my relatives there attested to that. I knew that it had never occurred to me to hate Jews—the memory of all the Jewish boys and girls who had shared my childhood in Cairo flooded over me—and that the distinction between Zionism and Judaism was very clear in my mind. I had, of course, no way to prove any of this. Looking back on it now, I believe I put up a brave fight, but the battle was lost before it began.

I had no dates, no names, no maps, no newspaper clippings with which to parry theirs. I was in fact very ignorant of politics and would probably have remained so had this episode and a thousand like it never occurred. By sheer necessity, I had to think about things I would probably never have thought of unprovoked and to argue a case that, the greater the blind opposition to it, the clearer it became to me and therefore the more compelling.

Later, reeling from the bitterness of the experience, I went to the library and studied modern history from an altogether new viewpoint. I read about the Ottoman Empire and the first stirrings of modern Arab nationalism; I read about McMahon's dealings with Hussein, promising independence to the Arabs if they helped in the fight against the Ottomans; I read about how, while these promises were being made, Sikes and Picot, complicit in imperial treachery, were already dividing up the map of the Arab world; I studied the Balfour Declaration and its background and development; I read about the beginnings of the Zionist movement, read Herzl and others; I followed the strain through the two World Wars and the final accomplishment of Israel. I read diaries and journals, books, and newspapers; I was determined never again to be caught unawares. I had been ashamed of my own ignorance and was resolved to overcome it. At last, I understood what had happened in Palestine: the dates, the names, the places, the letters, the declarations, the promises, the lies, the tragedies, I knew them all. Now I could argue and was convinced that reason, logic, and historic proof were all that had been lacking. I believed that my failure had been mine alone and that, if only I had been better prepared, they would have understood everything.

The bitterest discovery of all was that, in spite of the knowledge I aquired of dates and names and places, in spite of the logic of history now at my beck, I was no better off in later arguments. This kind of hostility, it seems, is not vulnerable to proof or argument. It is based on something mysterious and intangible, closely akin to myth, which is immune to reason.

I was to remain in America for more than ten years beyond college. After receiving my BA, I was married in Beirut. I had met my husband in Dhour el Schweire, my grandmother's mountain village in Lebanon, where we used to spend our summers. His family's summer house was close to ours, and our parents were old friends. Immediately after our marriage we returned to the United States, to live in a suburb of Washington, DC. My husband went to work for an international organization, and I did graduate work in English literature. It was here that our sons' earliest childhoods were spent.

Living in America in the 1960s meant living in turbulent and exhilarating times. The civil rights movement, the Vietnam War and the protests against it, the feminist movement, and the space shots—all these were happening then. For me, this time was formative of many of my later attitudes.

Of the obsessive themes of those days, the demand for justice by blacks was perhaps the most powerful. I followed the debate between those who argued that the goal could only be achieved through violence and those who believed in nonviolence. I saw the rise and fall of the Black Panthers, the murder of Malcolm X, and later the murder of Martin Luther King. I saw the riots that followed, and the faces of the racists and their snarling dogs. Forever more I shall think of racism in terms of that elemental image. I saw the great marches and heard the great speeches; I read widely in the literature of the black movement. It became for me an archetypal example of the principle of which my father had often spoken: "You must stand up and fight for what you believe." People were fighting for justice against amazing odds, changing the world in spite of itself.

The Vietnam War came into my living room on television, as did the protest movement that it generated. I watched the grotesque brutalities of war, as well as the protests. I read widely in the polemics of the time, and it was then that I came to the conclusion that no argument under the sun could justify the unspeakable cruelty of any war.

As the feminist movement erupted, I attended lectures and had heated discussions with other young mothers on the nature of our lives and expectations. I read, and I debated, and I watched as some of my friends and contemporaries fell prey to the new ideologies—their old, traditional unthought-out attitudes smashed by new insights. While for me the ideas were not new, the passion and generalization of them were, and I was entirely caught up in them.

Through all of this, several things became clear to me. If the world was not a just one, justice could be and must be actively sought. If the human race was capable of the most appalling injustices, then it was also capable of the most glorious battles against them. If one set of weapons were bombs, guns, and knives, then another, as powerful, were words and reason. If blind prejudice could lead to boundless hatred and murder, then solidarity and faith in justice could destroy it.

There could hardly be a question at the time that justice was being pursued and was on the advance; that goodness was overcoming evil; that peace was supplanting war; that idealism was advancing against racist, sexist reaction; that science and rationalism were on the march—and that all of this was happening in the United States.

How much more terrible, therefore, and confusing was it for me when, in 1967, the war in the Middle East produced an outburst of cultural hatred unprecedented in my experience. The defeat of the Arab armies by Israel was greeted not as a historical or political event but as a moral one, as the triumph of a cultural entity over a brute force. While this view was in keeping with the generally moralistic tone of the time—always in danger of lapsing into cliché—scarcely an effort was made by even the most sophisticated public commentators, including those backing the civil rights and antiwar movements, to see the situation in its historical context or to sort out the strands of the conflict. The same groups that vociferously supported the demand for justice in America often seemed oblivious to the parallel Arab demands for justice; then inexplicably greeted a military occupation as a triumph of the spirit. The Arabs were portrayed as an evil, cruel, violent lot, whose battle against the Israelis was prompted by nothing more than anti-Jewish hatred and a natural enmity toward all civilized values. The story of Palestine, of the unjust dispossession of its people was entirely ignored. Arab and Islamic history and culture in their wide variety—science, poetry, philosophy, mysticism, architecture—were reduced to nothing and denied, represented as timelessly propelled by a single motive: wiping out the Jews, who had triumphantly foiled the sinister designs on their very existence. In this representation, there was confusion between Arab demands for justice and Nazi persecution of the Jews; civilization itself was seen as having been rescued by the gallant Israeli army, as though in some mysterious way it had retroactively undone history.

Standup comedians and talk-show hosts made jokes about the defeated armies, and their audiences responded with sidesplitting laughter. Political cartoonists used a stock figure to represent Arabs in general and their leaders in particular: a caricature with a large hooked nose, beady eyes, and a cruel posture—ironically similar to the old anti-Semitic portrayal of

Jews. Arab dress, the *kaffiyeh* and *igal*, the *abayyah* became emblematic of all that was hateful and outlandish. This was a declaration of war on an entire culture and I was stunned by it.

For me, the nadir of the experience came the day that Jerusalem was conquered by the Israelis. The news commentator's face appeared on the television screen. He was in shirtsleeves, tieless. His announcement was too important to delay, and he was in far too great a hurry to spread the glad tidings to bother with more formal attire.

Elated, he seemed to see himself as an electronic angel in an electronic Bethlehem. "Jerusalem," he declared, joyfully, "ladies and gentlemen, Jerusalem has been liberated!"

Liberated? Liberated from whom? By whom? Which enemy of this man had occupied the place that it should now be liberated? Which tyrant had been overthrown from whom it had now been liberated? And who were those noble liberators who had freed Jerusalem from its captivity? What battle was being referred to, and what historical framework was being invoked?

Sitting today in Beirut, so many years later, I ask myself whether that foolish man who celebrated the "liberation" of Jerusalem is celebrating still. Have his eyes been opened a little since then? Has he been watching the consequences, the pain since that wretched Jerusalem has been liberated? The tears of Jerusalem have spilled over and flooded Beirut, and Jerusalem and Beirut are sister cities in agony. Jerusalem is the vertical line, Beirut the transverse: Together they form the cross that we carry today.

In all my time in America, I formed many friendships and came to admire much that I saw. Even during that difficult time in 1967, many were the people who listened and asked questions. I was invited to a suburban church or two to tell the other side of the story; and I gave brief, informal lectures on the modern history of Palestine. The most serious problem I encountered was overcoming the fear of good people that, in listening to an Arab point of view, they might be guilty of associating with a Nazi sympathizer, on which point I had constantly to reassure them. I especially came to admire, even to love, those who were always willing to give money to good causes; whose walking shoes were always ready to be slipped on for another march for justice. I remember, too, those individuals in suburban churches who genuinely struggled with questions of faith. Their struggle was often personal, although they did have some social issues to argue over; and I believe many of them participated in the marches on Washington.

This refreshingly pure belief in goodness—perhaps exclusively American—the belief that one can set out to make the world a better place, was most impressive.

Here, in Beirut, in this morass of religious feuding—where faith itself seems to be the least important detail in the picture, where even those who believe that some action must be taken toward justice and peace cannot believe in the ultimate triumph of their own individual efforts—this simple optimism, the assurance that it is in one's power to change the world seems an enormously important weapon that has been lost.

4

In 1972 my husband accepted a teaching post at the American University of Beirut. We sold our house and moved to Beirut, which at the time was at its peak as a financial, educational, intellectual, political, social, and tourist center in the area. We had high hopes then that, even while we enjoyed the pleasurable social life here, we could contribute to the improvement of the social fabric, of the intellectual and educational life of the country. We never dreamed then that the catastrophe around the corner would occur; and even those who predicted some sort of trouble never imagined that it would take such dimensions.

For my husband, going to Beirut meant going home and picking up the strands of his life that he had left behind: There had never been any question in his mind but that he would go back. For me, never having lived here, coming to Beirut meant a hope that I, too, could make a home, could settle down completely and finally. It seemed easy to imagine I could do so, as so many of the contradictions that I had experienced in my life seemed to have been resolved here. West and East seemed to enjoy a peaceful coexistence. In my childhood that happy state had prevailed in my own little world but was unreal, an imagined harmony that did not really exist. Here in Beirut it seemed to occur in reality, and my search for a comfortable modus vivendi between the two cultures seemed to have been accomplished.

Beirut was a center, some would say the center, of the Arab world. At the same time, Western culture was probably more widely represented here than anywhere else in the region. American and French schools taught Arabic and Arab history, and national schools taught English and French. Europeans and Americans, Africans and Asians, were everywhere to be seen along with people from all over the Arab and Muslim world. The regional headquarters of most of the international press was here. The theaters and cinemas alternated Arabic films and plays with Western ones. Mosques and churches stood literally side by side. The Palestine cause was accepted as a just one by everyone, including the foreigners. People spoke Arabic, English, and French, among other languages; and the same tables boasted Western and Lebanese cuisine. There was a free press, and political ideas of all sorts were tossed about and argued over publicly and without inhibition. The schools and universities were the best in the region, and so were the hospitals: The staffs of these institutions included Arabs and foreigners. The annual arts festival which took place in the splendid temples of Baalbek featured the greatest musicians, dancers, and actors in the world, and among the high points of each season were performances by leading Arab singers, such as Um Kulthum and Fairuz, as well as an always sold-out performance of folk dancing.

Seventeen religious groups, including different Muslim and Christian sects and a not insignificant Jewish one, flourished here. The confessional system on which political life was based, and which apportioned political power on a sectarian basis, seemed to be on the wane and was, in any case, felt to be an artificial one. The population lived heedless of its sectarian divisions: Thus, a family would always count among its friends members of other sects; and visits exchanged at the various festival times were firmly established social customs. Everyone went to everyone else's funerals and weddings, joining in whatever rites were dictated then. Intermarriage between members of different sects was not uncommon. Many secularists looked forward to the day that seemed inevitably approaching when the confessional political system would be abolished altogether.

Social life combined the famous generosity of Arab hospitality with cosmopolitan sophistication. The conservative mores of the region were tempered by exposure to the more liberal West, and a happy medium was found. Family life, of course, was at the center of everything; and the emotional security of the extended family, which included at its fringes lifelong friends, made for comfort in times of trouble.

I do not mean to suggest an ideal existence, nor to diminish the importance of those problems that exploded so ferociously later—far from it. Yet to leave out the wealth of hopeful possibility in that society would be to deny an aspect of the terrible sadness and sense of waste at its loss that I feel today.

Even so, almost from my arrival I was struck by the flagrantly obvious contrast between rich and poor. The existence of a large middle class, by far the widest class in the structure, did nothing to disguise the vast inequities on either end of the scale. These two segments of the population were so visible—the one with its conspicuous consumption, the other with its slums—as to make each entirely aware of the other's existence. There was no one in the middle class who did not feel uneasy about this situation.

I remember one night feeling the repressed energy of the city's underlife. It was New Year's Eve, 1974. We were not participating in the evening's celebrations as my husband was in bed with the flu. I stood on my balcony and watched crowds of young men—the female presence was conspicuously absent—flowing by. They were doing no mischief, merely blowing whistles and horns, beating on the tin trash baskets that in those days hung on the streetlamps, and banging on the hoods of parked cars, laughing loudly and calling to each other—in general, making a terrific noise. They wore paper hats and threw streamers, often interspersed with cans and bottles picked up from the rubbish, thus burlesquing the more elegant parties that were taking place behind closed doors in homes and nightclubs throughout the city. I take no credit for second sight, but I felt a deep alarm that night, sensing that their celebration, although apparently good humored, was not entirely so; that the line between a laughing crowd and an angry mob was a fine one, and that it took the merest spark to transform one into the other.

It was not quite four months later that the war began; and I presume that many of the young men who fought and looted and caused the initial destruction were among those I had watched that New Year's Eve. Although it is true that, especially in the early days of the war, there were some clearcut issues, clashes of ideologies and nationalisms, I think there was also a spilling out of a generalized rage, a collective frustration that continues to this day and perhaps has even increased. Perhaps many of the young men who wield the guns do so to vent a bottomless anger with a world that has done them no good and, when they shoot, aim at their own dissatisfaction as much as at any more precise target.

There were many other things which discomfited me, but I had little time to articulate thoughts on them before we were caught up in the war. It seemed simple at first, and limited, but gradually grew in complexity to encompass every aspect of life and thought, even as it grew geographically and in intensity. Expanding ripples of conflicts in a lake of violence caused parallel ripples in my own existence, and sent me, reeling, fragmented portions of consciousness.

Gradually, I saw unraveling those different cultural strands that I had thought could be neatly knitted together. I saw some of the contradictions of my own upbringing and experience, as well as new ones, emerging to confront one another here; and found myself overcome by the effort to manage both the inner and the outer battles. Almost every aspect of the war I had fought out in my own heart. Whenever I heard the argument of one side expounded, I could immediately anticipate the other; and one without the other would seem to me simplistic, false. I could therefore accept and reject simultaneously all the arguments of the war, while at the same time categorically rejecting the war itself.

□

When I arrived in Beirut it was a great relief to me to be now in a place in which the modern story of Palestine was not only known and accepted, but identified with by everyone of my acquaintance. I no longer had to feel the need constantly to explain, or to be on guard against the insidious prejudices which had so often spoiled moments of my time in the United States.

My comfort was shortlived, however. While the vast majority of the people identified with the Palestinian cause, the increasingly felt presence of armed Palestinian groups, poised for their fight with Israel, added further tension to the already charged atmosphere in Lebanese politics. The Palestinian presence was particularly alarming to those who saw themselves as the defenders of Lebanese sovereignty—which was being corroded, in their view, by the Palestinians—and as the most important link to Western culture, which they also felt was being threatened. In the ensuing struggle, the Palestinians were heavily backed by the Lebanese left, principally by Muslims but also by many Christians opposed to the existing system and especially the predominant Maronite role in it. They saw in the PLO a revolutionary spearhead to help them change the system.

On April 13, 1975, an unsuccessful attempt was made on the life of Pierre Gemayel, a Maronite leader and founder of the Phalangist Party that had established a military arm. A few hours later, a bus full of Palestinians driving through the suburb of Ain-Al Rummanneh was ambushed and twenty-six people on board were killed. An armed battle took place and the Lebanon war was on. Initially, the war pitted Maronite fighters against Palestinians, but eventually the conflict widened and battles were fought between a growing number of militias on both sides.

For me, the growing and violent divisions between Lebanese and Palestinians made a wrenching and tragic spectacle. I felt committed to the demand for restitution and justice that the Palestinians were pursuing. At the same time, I felt that—in spite of the anachronistic political system, of the growing gulf between rich and poor; in spite of the need for a thousand urgent reforms—there was something of great value in Lebanon, above all, I think, the general climate of tolerance.

There should have been no contradiction between Palestinian and Lebanese interests. Quite the contrary. It seemed to me then and it seems to me still that it was precisely the relative humaneness of Lebanon that made it the natural setting for the

Palestinian effort to reclaim justice; and that by assisting in that effort, Lebanon would have fulfilled its own destiny. In my mind, they belonged together, these two forces, and I refused for years to see them as mutually exclusive. In fighting each other, each force betrayed not only the other but itself as well.

My heart sank further and further over the years as it became clearer that the Lebanese and Palestinian causes, from being wide expressions of a common humanity, were being squeezed into the narrow molds of exclusive nationalisms that were inevitably, it seemed, bent on a collision course that neither might survive.

And it was in the end the people on both sides, the unarmed ordinary people, who paid the price of this collision and all the other conflicts of the war.

As the war progressed and became more and more complicated, its description as a "civil war" between "rival Muslim and Christian factions" came to seem simplistic. This description left out ideological, class, regional, and international differences, not to mention many internal, fraternal quarrels. Still, like many clichés, it was based at least partly on the truth; and, however reluctantly, a religious conflict must be acknowledged to have occurred.

The religious aspect of the war was a particularly complex one. It could be seen as an offshoot of the Lebanese–Palestinian conflict, since those who most resented the Palestinian presence were Maronite Christians and since the vast majority of Palestinians were Sunnite Muslims. There are those, on the other hand, who would say that the Lebanese–Palestinian conflict was merely a reflection of the internal divisions between Christians and Muslims, without which the Muslims of Lebanon would never have turned to the Palestinians for help in changing the system. The Palestinian–Israeli conflict, of course, also had an important religious dimension to it, which was at the basis of all the other conflicts, the Jewish exclusivism of the Israelis being the great issue. On another level, and as time passed, the growing area of conflict could be seen as including a cultural war between East and West, a modern replay of the Crusades; with the West, in its capacity as defender of Israel, once again represented as an aggressive force trying to dominate an Arab, or Muslim, world.

In any case, over the years, a terrible series of forced evictions of whole segments of the population occurred in Lebanon, and, as a result, the country became more and more religiously segregated.

In all of this, I have felt repeatedly that religion has worked rather like the stamp with which cattle are branded. I have seen it so many times in the movies. The cowboy chases the steer relentlessly. He throws a noose over the animal's head, tightens his hold on its neck, kneeling over the struggling body; and at last, in the single moment of its passive surrender, brings the hot iron into contact with the brown skin. A sizzle is heard, signifying at once conquest and submission, and then an agonized scream. His task accomplished, the cowboy, in one quick careful move, loosens the rope and his clutch, jumping away from his angry victim as it struggles back to its feet and takes off in furious rejection. Grim satisfaction is, however, on the man's face; for, like it or not, and all its struggles notwithstanding, the steer has been branded.

And so are we all, like it or not, branded with the hot iron of our religious ancestry. Believers and nonbelievers alike, struggle though we may, we are being corraled into the separate yards of our fellow coreligionists by the historic events of the moment. Belief and political vision have less to do with how one is seen, and then is forced to see oneself, than with external identification—the brand.

Although I am, by this definition at least, a Christian, I think of Islam as part—a large part—of my heritage and revere it as such. The Muslim past is my past and I am tied up with it. I am the child in equal measure of Christianity and Islam, but, to my great discomfort, the marriage made between them in my historical background is threatened. I do not wish to choose between them. Yet the choice is being made for me by elements over which I have no control, because of the transformation of spiritual, cultural qualities into political, military, demographic ones. The situation I find myself in is like that of watching the rape of my own past, two legs of one body being forced apart to the eternal shame of victim and violator.

It has often been said that the genius of the Middle East is a religious one and that it found its expression in Judaism, Christianity, and Islam. But of the wide and noble heights of the human spirit that these embody there is little trace to be found in the narrow and militaristic interpretations of the moment.

Thus the most atrocious crimes have been committed in the name of religion. Golden symbols have hung around merciless necks as slaughter was done and cities and villages were destroyed. I refuse to play the game of numbers: "Who did it more to how many?" is an immoral question. "Who did it first? Who started the vicious game?" That, too, is an immoral question. To raise the question is to imply that to have been second is to have been, somehow, less guilty. But these are the questions that people have been asking.

And how does the brand work? How does one fall into the clutches of that cowboy holding the hot iron? How does one feel as it sizzles into the flesh? I have felt it at moments—in conversations, perhaps, or through accusations that, thrown out carelessly, included me and forced my denial and therefore anger. Sometimes a fleeting impression could call the entire history and meaning of religion into question. Sometimes a nostalgic memory could do the same. However, it is clear that part of one's identity is created as the brand sizzles, struggle and kick though one may.

Item: People use the word *Christian* too often when referring to certain political parties. I squirm. It is not the same, you know: Political ideology and religious, cultural heritage are two different things. The same, of course, is true when people speak of the Muslims. For years, foreign journalists spoke of "Christian rightists" and "Muslim leftists," and we chided them for their simplistic reduction of complicated history to these clichés in which we were caught, branded.

Item: We would often cross over from "Muslim West Beirut" to "Christian East Beirut." Grudgingly, I have to admit it— the east was cleaner, more orderly, pleasanter in a middle-class sort of way, than the west side. Yes, but at what cost? The "Christian" area was created by the forcible eviction of those who were not considered acceptable. There were no slums or refugee camps here to offend the sight or oppress the spirit or threaten their surroundings: The ones that had been here were razed to the ground and their former locations "sanitized." In Jounieh, fashionable shops and restaurants were growing in number every day. The cinemas were clean and luxurious and showed the latest films. People were well dressed and well groomed in these places, the air redolent with *Eau Sauvage* and *Opium*, not with the stink of rotting garbage as it was in the west. Shopping arcades sprang up here in the latest European style, while ugly shacks were springing up on the west side. The names of many shops and restaurants imitated Parisian establishments.

Is this what it is all about? one wanted to ask those who have defended this vision of history. Is this the Christian heritage? The Garden of Gethsemane and Golgotha—where are their traces to be found in this citadel to the bourgeois spirit? Is this what thousands of people have died for—a sparkling shopping arcade and an expensive restaurant?

And yet, let us be fair. There have been bishops and patriarchs, priests and monks, who have refused all of this, who have called for the faith to be restored in its proper form.

There have been teachers and shopkeepers, taxi drivers and housewives, peasants and landlords who have refused. Besides, there are large numbers of poor people here, living hard, miserable lives, without assistance or benefit of the system that is supposed to favor them.

I was always relieved to get back to the smelly, bustling, overcrowded, ugly west side of the city. It is real and full of life. Not that there were no fanatics here: There were and are still. But there is a mixture of peoples, and it is the mixture that is beautiful and holy, unlike the holiness of either side that has caused so much suffering.

The mixture is threatened. In the west side, Christians have been kidnapped and killed, their shops blown up. Whole regions in the mountains and in the south have been emptied of their Christian inhabitants, many killed, the rest evicted. Villages were destroyed, sometimes razed to the ground.

And yet, let us be fair. Church bells ring on Sunday still. Sheiks, scholars, taxi drivers, housewives, shopkeepers, students renounce the violent, segregating acts. There is a large Christian community in West Beirut, not as large as it once was and not entirely at ease, but still there, still affirming its faith in the mixture.

Item: After the Israelis pulled out of the Shouf mountains in 1983 following the invasion, a series of interconfessional massacres took place. Christians murdered Druses, and Druses murdered Christians. The immensity of these crimes lies not only in themselves but in their implications. I can refuse to do it but I cannot refuse to have it done to me. Nor can I refuse to have it done in my name, refuse though I will. I am therefore caught in a terrible trap. There is no longer any question of logic, of will, of belief, of choice: There is only the brand.

Item: In 1979, Khomeini triumphs over the Shah. There is great rejoicing, disproportionate rejoicing, in Beirut. What does it mean? Everyone is pleased at the demise of tyranny. Why, then, the discomfort in some circles? Nationalism and religion are mixed together in a muddy puddle. Rejection of Western imperialism is coming to mean rejection of the West and everything in it, including Christianity; it means the acceptance of a purely Islamic past. How, if you are not a Muslim? How, even if you are and want to embrace not the past but the future? How, if you refuse the idea of Christianity as exclusively a Western imperial phenomenon?

One night, soon after the Iranian revolution, there was a heated discussion in our house between two friends of ours not previously acquainted with one another. I listened, gripped. The Muslim said to the Christian: "Why should you feel threatened by an Islamic republic? When has Islam ever been anything but the most tolerant of religions? Where can you find in your violent Christian history a parallel to the tolerant heights of the Islamic empire, in which Jews and Christians were protected? Was it not the Christians in Spain who, after the fall of the empire, persecuted both Muslim and Jew?" Her answer: "True, all true. I do not deny the tolerance of the Muslim past. I do not deny that a future Islamic entity might be as tolerant. But I do not wish to be simply not persecuted. I do not wish to be suffered to practice my religion or even to exist simply as an aspect of your tolerance. I refuse this sufferance. I wish to be a modern citizen of a modern state, with full political and civil rights second to no one else's."

Item: A Maronite friend is furious every time the word *Maronite* is used as synonymous with *Phalangist*, or even as suggesting a monolithic response. When rich Muslims or Druses with powerful family connections speak of their own oppression (their reference is to the confessional system), many middle-class or poor Christians become apoplectic.

Item: It is the funeral of a third cousin of mine. We are at the

Greek Catholic Church of Peter and Paul in West Beirut. To one side of me sits, stands, obedient to the rites, an elderly Druse lady of my acquaintance. To the other, sits my Greek Orthodox neighbor. Nearby is Dr. A, a Shiite, with his wife at his side, standing now and sitting, obedient to the rites. There is a Maronite I know and there a Sunnite.

In the underground shelter, I have sat with people of all religions and nationalities. We have comforted each other, shared food, water, blankets, candles.

This has been a single, though diverse community. This has been the reality. This is what is being threatened: An enormously rich cultural and human experience is threatened with fragmentation and sterile separation.

In spite of all that has happened, in spite of the viciousness and cruelty, the vast majority of the people reject the religious divisions that have spread like a terrible cancer. The tumor has grown—there is no question about that—and the whole organism is threatened. Religious fanaticism every day raises its ugly head around us. But every time it is perceived there is a rejection of it, sometimes public and loud, sometimes whispered and implied. There is hope in this reaction that the disease may yet be conquered. It takes one madman to frighten the consciences of a thousand people and lead them, even, to acts of hatred. Against this, as against violence, there is no use in argument, only in flat out rejection, and refusal. Courage may be found yet, and everyone may find there is more to be feared in submission than in refusal.

The worst danger of all, in this bloodbath into which we have been plunged, is not the loss of life, but the loss of faith. I don't mean loss of faith in God: I mean loss of faith in humanity and in each other.

□

The religious dimension of the conflict reflected on many social ideas, including the question of women. Within any culture, which social idea has been more debated in recent times? How much more problematic is it therefore here? Although there is an important feminist movement based in the Islamic and Arab tradition, the recent religious revival has raised the old issues and worried many women here. The complexity of the matter was well illustrated to me a few years ago, well before the Islamic revival had reached the peaks it was to attain later, at a lecture I attended in the college where I teach.

The lecture was part of a course on cultural issues and was given by an American woman. Although she had lived in Beirut for years, she had been immured in an academe whose ancestry was American and which had not yet made the serious concessions to local culture that the war and its consequences would require within a few years. Her lecture was put together with that enthusiasm for feminism that was still fresh in the West. She quoted from all the best writers: Simone de Beauvoir, Germaine Greer, Kate Millett. She said all the right, if by then a little hackneyed, things in just the right order.

Why then did I squirm so in my seat as she spoke? Why was I overcome by a terrible sense of the ridiculous? Why the nagging sense of indecorous intrusion, the discomfort of seeing a perfectly intelligent woman tampering with something about which she understood nothing—missing the point, somehow?

Certainly it was not for any lack of enthusiasm on my part for the feminist movement. Nor that it wasn't time for women here to revolt. It was high time. Nor that there were not certain universal aspects to the oppression of women: I have lived in both worlds, and I know there are.

What then?

I think it was that she had produced not an argument

based on the real experience of women here but an ideology ready for immediate consumption, and was oblivious to the difference. Like all ideologies, this one sprang out of certain conditions in a given culture. In the West the question of women was waiting to be picked, like a ripe fruit off a tree. So many other issues had already been dealt with—from the secularization of society, through revolutions and reforms of several hundred years, not to mention recent advances in science and medicine. The tree had been nourished and sprayed, watered, and, in general, properly tended. Recognition of women had become the obvious next step, necessary not only for the fruit but to the tree's very existence.

Here, on the other hand, the question of women lies at the bottom of things and cannot be touched without upsetting the whole order. To put it another way and to bring the question up to date with events here, to discuss it is to open a wasp's nest of unresolved and disputed issues to which it is, by its very nature, related. Can the question of women be separated from religious arguments? Can it be separated from social or cultural ones? Is there not a connection between class oppression and the oppression of women? Are Western and Eastern values not at cause here? Are all these issues not the ones over which a war is being fought? And are women not often the symbols of the issues?

If it is impossible to tell a man's political beliefs from his clothing, it is relatively easier to tell a woman's. Militiamen all look alike: Regardless of which side they are on, they wear similar uniforms and carry similar weapons. Their wives and daughters, on the other hand, do not look alike. From the bikini to the *chador* lies a range of clothing that bespeaks a parallel range of belief and action. And yet, while perhaps nothing has created as much passion as the sight of the *chador* on the streets of Beirut or the bikini on the beaches, nothing is as easily misunderstood or as prone to simplistic interpretation as these items of clothing. For, if the *chador* is taken to be symbolic of a woman's submission, can it not also be symbolic of political rebellion and protest? And if the bikini has been considered symbolic of an open, forward look, can it not also be one of mindless, backward-looking decadence? Furthermore, two women wearing their *chadors* do not necessarily have identical views on things, and neither do two women wearing bikinis. Yet, within the bounds of common sense and reason, it is possible to identify them roughly with widely disparate visions of the world.

Pending the resolution of the issues being fought over and while the war continues, women have lived their lives in as many ways as it is possible to imagine. And pending the time when the question can be discussed within a rational framework, rather than in the whirlpool of violently conflicting currents, I find myself retreating and thinking of the status of women in a tranquil, reflective way.

If I were giving the lecture, then, how would I do it? I think probably I would simply offer a small image, a memory that has been tucked away in a corner of my mind for years. I have often taken it out and looked at it, savoring its meaning, then quietly packed it up again, as one does a souvenir from a journey taken long ago:

The little girl traipses behind an adored big brother through the woods. The quiet is broken by the sound of their feet trampling the dried pine needles of high summer in the mountains of Lebanon. He kicks away an occasional stone, and she, in loving imitation, kicks it again. Here and there, an old can lies rusting in a thicket under a thorn bush. To make their way, they have to push aside low branches that sometimes scratch their faces and hands. When they emerge in a clearing, the sun is scorching, and they tug at the little cotton caps that protect their heads from its heat, wiping from their brows beads of sweat, and leaving there muddy streaks.

They do not talk. He, much bigger than she, is several

strides ahead, and she has to skip and run a few steps every now and then just to keep him in sight. He has suffered her to accompany him on this walk and she glows with the honor of his condescension.

He is fourteen or fifteen years old, approaching manhood, which he is trying out. He is carrying a shotgun, and his eyes are searching out birds. Hunting is a sport for which he has no taste, but he feels it incumbent on him to practice it, as it is part of the path that has been prepared for him by the generations preceding him. It is an initiation ritual, something he simply must do.

He finds his target, kneels in the dirt, takes aim and fires. At the crackle of the gun, she hides her face, and her dirty hands instinctively go up to cover her ears. He, no less frightened or horrified, watches with fascination as a bird falls out of a tree and lands with a gentle thud a few yards ahead. She raises her head, watching him, and together they take a few steps towards the small dead body. They stand together, looking down at it silently, mourning. Finally he straightens up, slings the gun onto his shoulder and walks away, looking for his next victim.

She watches him go, then looks down again at the dead bird. This is the moment she has been dreading: The task is now hers. This is the price she has to pay for his august company.

She stoops down and picks up the body. It feels warm and damp and soft in her trembling fingers. When she gets home later, she will wash her hands again and again, but like Lady Macbeth, she will be unable to clean away the ghastly, sticky feeling.

Controlling her desire to retch, quelling that part of her that refuses to do what she has to do, distancing her consciousness, she attaches the little carcass to the empty clip dangling from the belt around her waist. It is not easy: The limp body resists the firm clutch of the steel. She has to push and pull; every nerve in her body tingles with horror, until finally the neck of the bird is secured in the grasp of the hook. There is some blood on her hand, and in desperate haste, she bends and wipes it in the dirt, rubbing and rubbing, until her skin is raw. So intent is she on getting off the blood that she does not at first notice the body of the bird pressing on her thigh. The instant she does, she leaps up and turns the belt, first this way, then that. But no matter how she turns it, she still feels the corpse against her body.

She looks around for her brother, at first not seeing him; then, when she finds him, runs in his direction, relieved. In the pleasure of seeing him again, she forgets for an instant her unhappiness and calls his name. He turns on her in impatience: She has spoiled his aim and the bird has flown away. Perhaps he is relieved that it has. Yet he knows that he must now go through the painful process of finding another, tracking it down, and hardening his heart for what he must do.

After several hours, they go home. He still strides in front of her carrying the gun. She trails behind, all the dead birds now jostling against her thighs and sides, her blue jeans stained with their blood. He, not looking at them, presents his trophies in abashed triumph, pointing vaguely in her direction, then disappears into the house, rushing, she knows, to get first place in the bath that they both feel they desperately need. In the kitchen, she unfastens the belt and lays it on the table, a mound of leather and steel and balls of feathers and dead flesh.

Neither of them share in the meal that is presented that evening. In the neat rows of naked, fried birds lying, feet up, in the dish, they are haunted by the ghosts of the soaring, singing, feathered things that they have killed. They exchange a brief, painful glance, accomplices in murder. He responds glumly to the praises sung to his skill. No one mentions her as having had any share in the venture, and for a fleeting instant, she thinks to claim her part, wanting to protest that, after all, had it not been for her, there would be no supper tonight, just a lot of dead birds lying in the woods. But, protectively, she keeps her peace, a willing victim, but one who betrays him and her love for him merely by having that secret knowledge, by harboring that secret resentment.

☐

Almost all the arguments of the war, both those with which I have sympathized and those I have abhorred, have been played out in violence. There are those who argue that in a violent world, with violent oppressors and violent enemies, the only way to liberation is through the use of violence. Force, they argue, is the only language "they" understand, and therefore the only road to a better world. Clearly this is a very persuasive argument, for it has persuaded many people. Furthermore, there are those who argue that violence is in the nature of humanity, that it has always been and must always be; that it is a drive, an instinct as powerful as any other, that cannot be denied.

We who have not carried guns, who have refused to do so, are left with a little corner to stand in, a corner that sometimes seems to be the only one that counts and sometimes to be the most irrelevant, isolated, and inexcusably weak spot in the whole structure of the universe.

All my life, it seems, has been passed in the shadow of violence, and still I have no defense except outright rejection, no argument against it except to point at the desolation around me. What weapon is there but this, and of what use is this? Of all the hopeless battles ever waged, what could be more hopeless? Nothing but an accusing finger to oppose huge military establishments, to oppose the vast armaments industries, to oppose reams of philosophical and political and sociological arguments, to oppose human history itself.

Familiarity, they say, breeds contempt. Familiarity with violence breeds contempt—for what? People? Life? Nature? Goodness? Beauty? Prayer? God himself? For me, familiarity with violence has bred contempt for violence, and only for that, for I have seen what it has accomplished and it is nothing to be proud of.

If the war in Lebanon has come to mean anything to me, it is the putting out of lights; it is the corruption of cause after cause by the very arms that were meant to protect them. Ideals were once planted carefully in the earth, from which they were meant to spring in abundance and beauty, but their planting ground has become instead their burial place. The harvest is blighted, and we stand in a wasteland of empty words and meaningless gestures of violence. For in the end, a killing is a killing, and one bullet looks very much like another, and all of them whizzing about my ears make me want to stand up and scream *Enough. Enough.*

In the name of one sacred cause after another, whether national, cultural, political, religious, or simply the primeval cause of survival, stand such monuments to the spirit of sacred causes as have been erected in the mountains and cities and villages and refugee camps of Lebanon. In the name of causes come the screams of children, the wails of mothers, the smoke of a burned land. In the name of humanity comes the merciless inhumanity of air raids, tanks, machine guns, and throats slit from ear to ear gushing blood.

And in the midst of this orgy of violence, this dance of death, this saturnalia of killing, what is there to do but refuse it? Put it down, this refusal, if you will, to sentimental bourgeois finickiness, and dismiss it with contempt. I have no answer, except to say that I have seen what I have seen.

V

Summer, 1982:
The
Israeli Invasion

I T was Friday, June 4, 1982. There was to be an athletics awards ceremony at the International College, near the American University of Beirut. My youngest son, age eleven, was to receive an award for soccer. We had arranged that his brothers and I would meet him at the playing field after school and proceed to the ceremony. As I stood at the edge of the field beckoning to him, the war began. It was a little after three o'clock in the afternoon.

It took a few minutes for it to register in my mind that something serious was happening. The clear blue sky was being embroidered with the white lines left by the darting jets, their silver shapes gleaming as they dived, turned, dived again, and flew off, screaming, spewing their glistening missiles and heat balloons. In a few seconds the sky was dotted as well with the explosion of hundreds of anti-aircraft shells.

At first, the children on the soccer field, the teachers who had emerged from the school buildings, the bus drivers leaning against their green and white vehicles, other passers-by, and I stood, mesmerized, looking up at the planes.

For years the Israelis had been bombing Lebanon. Most often they bombed the south and then passed screaming over our heads here in Beirut. Sometimes they flew so low that their sonic booms shattered our windows, as they did our nerves. Usually they were fired at by anti-aircraft guns situated on the coast and near the Palestinian refugee camps. There was no possibility whatsoever that the Lebanese air force, such as it was, could offer the slightest challenge to the Israelis. Indeed, the air force and its antique planes were often the subject of cynical jokes among the population. Long ago, air raid sirens had stopped wailing at the Israelis' approach, and long ago the government had stopped issuing civil defense warnings of any kind, thus acquiescing to the inevitability of their passage. Civilians, especially outside the refugee camps, were on their own to make a decision about what precautions, if any, to take during the passage of the planes. Generally, people rushed out to their balconies or craned their necks on the streets to get a better look, pointing with strange fascination at the direction they had taken.

There was a peculiar relationship between Beirutis and the Israeli planes: If one dared, one might almost call it romantic. In this attitude was a strange commingling of repugnance and desire, alienation and belonging, intimacy and coldness. It was partly admiration for the breathtaking technology; for the sheer physical beauty of the gleaming, silver streaks in the clear blue skies; for their seductive elegance. Partly also it was the soaring sensation one felt as, fixed to the earth, one watched as they flew and turned, dived and soared again, extraordinarily free and graceful, unchallenged masters of the sky. There was a shared experience with them, the crucified and the crucifier united in those moments, in the possibility of godhead in us all, the taking of life and the suffering of sacrificial death, because always the death they delivered was perceived as sacrifice. In a sense there was in that foolhardy, neck-craning, finger-pointing refusal to take cover a kind of symbolic appropriation of the technology and mastery of those silver screams in the sky.

The attitude towards the planes betokened as well a kind of grudging admiration for the Israelis. They at least had succeeded where everyone else had failed. There we were, foundering in the violence that had plagued us all these years, and there were they, masters of the game, watching and recording our misery as they flew overhead year after year, mocking the threat of the anti-aircraft guns.

Always the Israelis announced that they had bombed "Palestinian targets" or "terrorist bases." Always there would be terrible anger and bitterness, not only at the raids themselves but at the hypocrisy of the announcements. If the targets were often Palestinian refugee camps, they were as often Lebanese villages; and if some fighters were killed, the majority of the victims in either case were civilians. The pictures in the papers were always the same: babies and old men, Palestinian and Lebanese, lying dead or dying; bits of bodies, shops, and cars; houses reduced to unrecognizable rubble; an old woman, wiping away her tears, picking her way through the ruins of her home, holding up a picture, perhaps, a saucepan, a bent and twisted vase—items that had once been part of her life and now had lost all meaning.

On this particular afternoon, boys, pointing at the sky, excitedly vied with each other to identify the planes. "That was an F15," one said. "No, a Phantom," said another. "Kfirs," insisted a third. The boys' attitude was not much different from their elders. It was as though the compensation for not owning such planes yourself lay in the ability to identify them.

By giving a plane a name you acquired some sort of relationship to it. And so we all stood and watched.

There was a certainty that day that the planes were not coming at us here in our haven of Ras Beirut. We all knew that their targets must be the Palestinian refugee camps on the outskirts of the city, so we could stand and watch with impunity. In fact, the danger that afternoon came, ironically, not from the planes themselves but from the shells fired at them; and several children were injured by the shrapnel falling out of the sky. By the time school officials had peremptorily shepherded everyone indoors, it was abundantly plain that this was not just another Israeli hit-and-run attack. In fact, the air raid lasted about two hours.

I stood inside the school building, surrounded by the sweaty bodies of dozens of boys, thankful that at least I was with my sons and didn't have to worry, as so many mothers did that day, whether they were safe, whether they were on the road, whether they were sensible enough to take cover.

Some of the younger boys in the crowded school corridor were visibly frightened and on the brink of tears. Some of the older boys, blasé and seemingly immune to fear after years of war, just carried on punching one another and making crude jokes about each other's awkward shapes. A pimply fifteen-year-old standing behind me chattered with his friend, his voice alternating between soprano and bass registers. "This must be," he croaked cheerfully, "their response to the shooting of the Israeli ambassador in London yesterday." Then he added acidly, "If they did all this for one ambassador, think what they would have done for two!"

In fact, for the next few days we were to hear a great deal about that ambassador. Although the PLO had denied responsibility for the shooting and, indeed, had roundly condemned it, Israel held the PLO responsible and, as usual, claimed the right of retaliation. After a while nobody mentioned the ambassador anymore, until—several tens of thousands dead later;

several hundred thousand refugees later; after large parts of Tyre, Sidon, Damour, and Beirut, not to mention dozens of other towns and villages had been destroyed—there was a small item in the newspaper that he had survived and been discharged from the hospital.

It was not until things had quieted down and we had scurried home, athletics awards forgotten, and turned on our radios that we knew just how serious this raid had been. There were hundreds of casualties and enormous material damage.

The day after the raid, June 5, was the fifteenth anniversary of the start of the 1967 war. Lunching with friends, we toasted the memory of that outbreak, typically mixing humor with bitterness. Each of us remembered our whereabouts and reactions in that dismal period, little guessing that in a few days 1967 would seem pale by comparison with 1982. As we discussed the previous day's air raid we argued about whether or not it would be repeated. Most of us felt it would not, as today was Saturday, the Jewish sabbath, and the previous air raid had ended just before sunset. Soon enough, however—the sabbath notwithstanding—we had to rush to the corridor several times and once even to the basement, as the Israelis resumed their attack. We made several attempts to leave the building, but each time had to rush back indoors as one sortie followed another. Finally, after a half-hour of quiet, we ventured on our way.

By noon of the next day, June 6, we knew that an invasion had begun in earnest. The Israeli army had crossed the border. At first, the number of troops mentioned was so staggering that we thought there must be some exaggeration in the reports. Since the Israeli evacuation from Sinai began to be discussed, and long before it actually took place, it was clear to everyone in Lebanon that the price for Egyptian peace would be paid here. A proverb had grown popular over the years: *Whenever the clouds gather in the Arab world, it rains in Beirut.* So at last, and to no one's surprise, it had come, just a few weeks after the withdrawal from Sinai, but the scale and scope of the invasion and the toll it would take had not been imagined.

That evening, we watched the television news, maps in hand. It had been announced from Israel that "the operation" was called "Peace for Galilee" and that the Israeli aim was to create a forty-kilometer "security zone" to protect the citizens of Galilee from "the terrorists" who had, just a few days before, shot the ambassador in London. Once more we were faced with Israeli claims of the need to secure its borders, of moral justification for the attack. In our own perception, Israel was an unshackled aggressor, being granted a moral cloak by the world's—at least the western world's—unquestioning acceptance of its claim to morality. In the West, its regularly recurring acts of violence seemed always to be regarded as aberrations.

After lingering on the immense damage caused by the air raids of the last three days, the news program showed an episode that demonstrated the irrelevance of all else to the actual experience of horror. The body of an Israeli pilot, killed in the crash of his plane, was in the hands of the people of a village in the south. They were beating it, kicking it, cursing, their faces distorted in rage. Sitting, horrified, in my still comfortable living room watching this frightful episode, I tried to switch off the set to prevent my children's seeing it. They showed a morbid curiosity—natural, I suppose to children of their ages—and insisted on watching. Finally, I gave in, feeling that they had been through so much war, had been at risk of losing their lives so often, that I had no right to censor even war's ugliest realities from their knowledge. We argued about the villagers' response. "What would you do if we had been killed?" they asked. "What if you had lost everything in an air raid?" "I hope," I said, "I hope I wouldn't do that."

No doubt the villagers had been restrained eventually,

and the body rescued from their hands; but who was I sitting comfortably in Beirut, to disapprove their reaction, their impotence in the face of the continuous Israeli air raids, destroying year after year their people, their homes, their crops, their lands, translated into this one mad gesture of revenge and hate? In the months that followed I was to think often of this episode.

That Sunday came the first warning to foreigners from their governments to leave the country. In all the crises of the past years, the barometer was precisely this action and so foreigners were often asked by Lebanese if they had heard from their embassies yet. That the warning this time should come on the first day of the invasion and from the United States—viewed always as the principal ally and defender of Israel—was seen by many people as an indication that something big was in store. As in all other households, the question was raised in my family about whether we should leave. I made a pact with my husband: This time, no matter what happened, I was not going to take the children and run. The only thing on my mind at this point was my experience in 1976. After several weeks of shelling following the wrecking of our home, I had taken the children away for what I thought would be a few weeks and had ended up staying away for eight wretched months. Long ago, with thousands of others, I had resolved that at times like these it is better to be on hand and to know what is happening than to be far away getting vague news piecemeal.

On Monday, June 7, we awoke to the news that there was to be no school for the boys, although the universities muddled on. At first final exams for schools and universities were postponed; later they were canceled altogether. Almost every school in West Beirut was eventually converted into a refugee center or a clinic; and the question arose, as the summer wore on, whether there would be a school year at all after the invasion. Still, teachers did manage to produce final grades for every student, and the academic year was, though abbreviated, completed.

On Tuesday afternoon, as a result of the Israeli air raids on Jiyyeh, south of Beirut, where a major power station lay, the electricity went off. The power was to be restored a day later but rationed; later, of course, during the siege, we learned to live without electricity at all. At this point, however, there was a flurry of emptying freezers that had been stocked just the day before in anticipation of possible food shortages. In the next few days, if one dropped by to see a friend and exchange news, one was inevitably offered hastily defrosted *fatayir, sambousik*, and *kibbe* with some desperation, so that there was an inappropriately festive feeling to such visits. Once more, people could be seen carrying plastic containers full of water from wherever they could get it: The first problem with the loss of electricity was always the consequent loss of water.

By the middle of the week, the Israelis had reached Sidon, and stories began to emerge of the horrors experienced in the south. For most Beirutis they were still just stories, and Beirut itself remained relatively unaffected but for the never-ending procession of planes overhead and a number of air raids on the outskirts of the city. The south was totally cut off from the rest of the world. No telephone lines functioned, and normally intrepid reporters could not make their way to or from the region. All we knew for sure was that first Tyre and then Sidon were being subjected to immense bombardments from land, sea, and air. Day after day the battles continued, and day after day people with relatives in the south became more and more desperate for news.

At one point, I went to see DJ. Her face was pale, and as soon as I asked her what news she had of her family in Sidon, tears welled in her eyes. She switched on the radio, which had been in her hands when I entered her office at the university, shrugged, and then switched it off again, hopeless. "I know as much as you do, and the radio is no help," she said. Her mother and brothers were in Sidon. She didn't know if they were alive or dead. If alive, how were they? Was their house still standing? Did they have food? Water? Was anyone wounded? If so, could they get to the hospital? Were the hospitals functioning? Nobody knew anything.

We heard that the International Committee of the Red Cross had asked the Israelis to stop the bombardment and agree to a truce, if only for a few hours, so that the wounded could be taken for treatment, so that supplies could be furnished, so that bodies could be removed—and the Israelis had refused. Televised interviews with officials of the Lebanese Red Cross and the Civil Defense Agency offered dreadful details of the casualty figures, and it was clear that many people who could have been saved would die.

One morning that week, R and T rang my doorbell. They had come to Beirut on vacation, having moved to Europe when the war began, and now were stranded. The airport was closed, as it would be for the next five or six months, and alternative routes had still not been arranged. "We can't just sit around listening to the radio," they said. "We must *do* something." By then, there were mass movements of people in Beirut. Many Palestinian refugees had fled the camps, which were being continuously bombed; those who lived in the same general area had also fled, and many people had moved to Beirut from the south, ahead of the invading army. Thousands of people were milling around, taking over empty flats wherever they could find them, settling into public gardens, schools, and mosques, and otherwise fending for themselves. Their situation was appalling. I agreed with R and T. We must do something, but what? Helping the refugees was not something that could be undertaken by a few well-meaning volunteers: We had neither the means nor the authority to deal with such a problem. The Red Cross and Civil Defense officers who had been interviewed on television had made it clear that their need was not for untrained volunteers, who would probably hamper their efforts, but for the permission to do the work that they could accomplish if only they could get to it.

Finally we thought we could be useful if we could organize a way to channel news of members of the scattered families to each other. We went to the Ministry of Information with our idea. It was immediately picked up and set into motion, but entirely without our help, so that we felt as useless as ever.

For weeks after that, you could hear on the state radio, in between news broadcasts, messages of reassurance sent by individuals to their families elsewhere in the country, most often in the south; or, more poignant, requests for reassurance from people who had totally lost touch with loved ones. Sometimes I sat and listened to the names being broadcast, trying to imagine the faces and experiences that went with them and wondering whether or not the messages were being received.

This episode made me feel the familiar sense of my own redundancy. The present reality made me, and thousands of others like me, look back over my life as at a prologue to a play that would never be acted, while the play in progress had been unrehearsed, undreamed of. Once more the failure of our society was clear: In the face of the cataclysmic events now unfolding, we were a totally immobilized population, totally unprepared, totally useless. Our individual talents, not inconsiderable, I think, were wasted, water trickling out of a thousand leaks in the pipe instead of pouring effectively into a useful flow.

The battles came to the outskirts of Beirut. From now on, the threat of the "Battle of Beirut" hovered over us, until suddenly we realized that it was no threat, that we had been in it all along.

And how to describe those battles? How to capture in words the horror of those weeks? The sky orange with the unnatural light of exploding phosphorus bombs; the whizzing screams of jets darting for the kill; the graceful beauty of the flares falling gently in the night sky, iridescent golden balls on black velvet, lighting the whole world, it seemed, their charm belying their murderous intent. And the sound of the battles—one eschews *thunder* and *rumble* as too easy, too weak, to express it. It was a sound seemingly made by all the devils in hell beating gigantic drums under the earth and over it; a sound like that of the sea breaking its bounds or of a frightful, rebellious monster hatched out of the shell of the earth.

I would have to tell also of the fear seeping in like slow poison, panic spreading noiselessly; of gunboats sailing by gracefully, insolently, on the calm blue waters; of the sudden whistle and crash of the shells they fired; of the mad scramble downstairs to dubious shelter; of poor jokes told to quiet the nerves; of the growing sense of finality and no escape. The experience of war is unique, and all else, civilization and custom, law, truth, lies—all else pales and becomes irrelevant.

The intensity of the attacks, the frequency of the air raids, the nature of the weapons, the sheer numbers and weights involved, were staggering in comparison with what we had experienced before. We listened angrily to news reports of debates in the United States about whether or not the wide use by Israel of cluster bombs was defensive and therefore legal. For once I found myself in agreement with rhetoric that had previously irritated me, and the accusatory word *genocide* no longer seemed exaggerated. There was no doubt in my mind that the Israelis wished to destroy not just an organization or just an army but to stamp something out entirely: principally, the idea of Palestine in the minds of Palestinians and their supporters.

Suddenly, on the evening of June 25, there was silence and a ceasefire was announced. We heard that Alexander Haig had resigned as the U.S. Secretary of State, and we rejoiced, thinking that his departure meant a change in American policy and that we would be spared.

But on Sunday, June 27, there was a sudden scream of a plane and then an explosion, and confetti rained out of the sky. The pernicious leaflets of the Israel Defense Forces, printed on pink, green, and yellow sheets, fell gaily all around, while people snatched at them, chasing them in the wind like children playing with soap bubbles. The message read:

> *To the citizens of Beirut: The Israel Defense Forces have not used all the means at their disposal to defeat the terrorists. Save your lives and the lives of your loved ones. Leave Beirut. The following roads are open—Save your lives.*

This tactic had already been practiced in Sidon. The humiliation of finding oneself in the position of wanting safety, but knowing one could have it only by the ignominious flight offered by the Israelis was a bitterness increased by the memory of the flight from Palestine a generation ago. The empty house, the abandoned field, the refugee carrying his life in a suitcase— these were the symbols not only of the Israeli presence but of our own impotence as well.

When I read the leaflet, a momentary fear was immediately overwhelmed by a tremendous anger. I would not go; no matter what, I would not go.

But I did. My husband insisted. Like so many Lebanese, he had learned the lesson of Palestine, and so he would stay; but for the safety of our children, I must take them and go. I argued; I pleaded; I fought; but he prevailed. Would I, he had shouted, would I take the responsibility if our children were burned like those we had seen on television the night before? The sight of those little burned bodies had made him vomit. I had not had the courage even to look at them.

I could not find a counterargument. "You take them; I'll stay," I had tried feebly. I had no right to condemn the children. I felt shame, humiliation, rage, as I packed in the dark—

there was no electricity that night—not knowing or caring what I threw into the accursed suitcase. My anger was a wheel with a hundred spokes: anger at my husband for forcing me to abandon my shortlived resolution, for breaking the pact that we had made earlier and which tonight he had waved aside as a piece of nonsense; anger at my children for the tyranny of their existence, to which mine was always secondary; at my friends for not supporting me in my stand, for themselves deciding to go; at my sister, who, triumphantly staying, had repelled my appeals with, "I haven't got children to think about"; at myself for not having the strength of my convictions; at the PLO and the Lebanese government for not ever, not even now, offering me a way out of this dilemma that they had helped create—for not making a suggestion, not denying, not denouncing, not asking for my support or help, not offering me a leg to stand on, for ignoring me, for not saying a word, for their silence in this most symbolic and awful moment; at the society in which I lived for leaving me out, so that just at this of all times I should have felt myself to be only a useless, discarded, redundant object, only another mouth to feed, another consumer of rapidly dwindling resources, another potentially wounded or dead body to heal or to bury—a nothing at all.

And so, on June 28, feeling betrayed and betraying, I left West Beirut to stay with friends on the other side. West Beirut was under the domination of the PLO and their supporters, while East Beirut was dominated by the Lebanese Forces who were at this point in direct collusion with the Israelis. This had, of course, only increased my reluctance to go.

Our friends had a house in the hills just above the city. Every house in the area was crammed with guests from West Beirut. For three weeks I sat there, ceaselessly listening to radio reports and playing "patience" with an old deck of cards, one of those things I had hastily thrown into the suitcase.

The fate of Beirut hung in the balance. The great question on everyone's mind was whether, having warned the civilian population to leave, the Israeli army was going to storm the city. Philip Habib, the American envoy, was shuttling endlessly back and forth to the Presidential Palace in Baabda and to the residence of the U.S. ambassador in Yarze. Shafiq al Wazzan, in his capacity as intermediary and Prime Minister of Lebanon, shuttled endlessly between meetings with the PLO and Philip Habib. While they talked, the battles continued.

Once in a while, I would take the children for a walk in those lovely hills. The roads were jammed with cars full of people from West Beirut, who, having no friends in the East and unable to afford the hotels, which were all full anyway, were camping in their cars. Some people had hitched up television sets to their car batteries and then, settling down comfortably, watched the World Cup soccer games. My children, soccer fanatics, would often join them, sitting on the rocks that lined the roads. On the evening of the finals, the war seemed to come to a complete stop: It was said that even the Israeli soldiers were watching the match, cheering the Italians on against the Germans.

Other people came in their cars and parked in the area for a different reason: This particular spot offered a panoramic view of Beirut, so they could watch the battles; a grotesque form of entertainment. Some evenings we would go up to the roof of our host's house and from there watch what was happening below: flares falling, rockets streaming red in the night sky, crisscrossing it in dozens of patterns, phosphorescent explosions rising silently, the sound following seconds later.

One day I drove up to Broumana to visit relatives and to buy some toothpaste. It was there, in the little village grocery store, that I saw my first Israeli soldiers. There, tucked away into the corner of my banal little task, was this confrontation, which became infected by the very banality that brought it about. Two young soldiers, rifles slung on their shoulders, were themselves buying little things—cigarettes, I think, and chewing gum. The huge refusal that welled in me was punctured, deflated by pettiness. I stared at them in disbelief, two rather shy young men, counting over the unfamiliar money with the cold assistance of the store's owners; then, flustered, choking on my own refusal, I left my toothpaste and fled, trying to look as though I were walking out in protest but in reality overwhelmed by the shame that had brought me together with them in mundane acceptance of the everyday needs we shared.

Looking back on this encounter today, I wonder if they were as trapped as I; if circumstances beyond their control had put them in the situation of murdering people, a people, while I had been trapped in the ignominy of being a mere spectator to my people's murder; both of us trapped and not trapped, doing what we were doing unwillingly but nonetheless doing it, acquiescing and therefore guilty. Did they, I wonder, eventually join the ranks of the brave young reservists who eventually protested against the war and the position into which they had been placed by it? Or did they act with the full conviction that they were doing the right, or at least the inescapable, thing?

In any case, at the time it happened, I suffered what might be called a moral vertigo. The Israeli army had invaded Lebanon with a brutality and ruthlessness that had already taken thousands of lives, Lebanese as well as Palestinian, and I had taken refuge in that part of the country dominated by those who were in collusion with the Israelis. I remembered a remark made laughingly by a friend years before, during the dark days of the civil war in 1976. "Did you hear?" he had said. "Did you hear what So-and-So said? Our situation is hopeless, but not serious." The situation, I felt now, might still be hopeless, but it had at last become serious. It was impossible now to sidestep the moral issue; to take neutral refuge meant to accept the Israeli violence. One either suffered from it, or allowed it; there was no middle ground.

One afternoon, I had a surprise visit from L and M. In the

early days of the invasion they had anticipated an Israeli attack on Beirut and had left the city for their house in their ancestral village of Bhamdoun. Bhamdoun, a town of great strategic importance dominating the international highway linking Beirut and Damascus, became the site of a great battle, and for days their friends were frantic for news of them. Finally we had a very brief and tense phone call. "We are alive," was all L could bring herself to say, her voice sounding strange and distant. "I can't talk anymore." After that we had heard nothing more of them.

Then, this particular afternoon, they tracked me down and came to call. She looked pale and thin. Her formerly long, black, glossy hair was cut short, her altered appearance accentuating the strangeness, the remoteness of her mood. In a dull, almost monotonous voice, she recounted to me what they had been through. They had been caught by surprise when the battle came. She had been in the village, shopping, and had had to take refuge in a shop for several hours. At one point there came a brief lull, during which she had made her way home, running through unfamiliar shortcuts and not sure, at moments, where she was. She reached home just as the battle was resumed with immense ferocity. As their house seemed to offer better shelter than most, several families joined them. They had had a bitter altercation with some of the fighters, whom they had requested not to place their guns so close to their house as to attract the Israelis. The fighters, who had no doubt met the same request from all the residents of the town, had refused to move. They were pinned down for hours as the battle reached its peak, and their house was very badly damaged by shells and bullets. Finally, in another lull at four o'clock in the morning, they had fled. She drove their car with thirteen people in it—as she told me this part of her story a faint smile appeared on her face, and she challenged me to get thirteen people into a car under normal circumstances. "I don't know how they fit, but they did." Her husband had driven his

Vespa—a very small motor bike—with another man behind him. They had rushed to Zahle, stayed there for a day or two, and then left it, this time only with their children. To get to East Beirut they had made a journey of five hours, taking the long road from the Bekaa through the Cedars and down to the coast again.

As she relived the battle in her memory, at odd moments fresh feeling seemed to penetrate; and planes, tanks, and great guns were all pounding the house again and she was again crouching in the corner, knowing they were all going to die. Sitting there in my host's garden, surrounded by geraniums and roses and fig trees, sipping tea, her experience seemed dreamlike, unreal.

Yet, I felt as though she had been through something that had changed her forever. The unfamiliar short hair, the quiver of her hand as she lit cigarette after cigarette, the dull monotone of her normally rich voice, the wooden, dazed expression on her normally lively face; all betrayed transformation. Her situation made mine even more intolerable to me.

It was not out of a spirit of masochism that I wished to experience what she had, but out of impatience and frustration with the sense of having been cast aside, of being on the outside fringe of things, of not living what I should be living—of having history, as it were, spilled on me rather than being able to drink from its bitter cup. More than ever, I wanted to go home.

My resolve was at last accomplished partly by chance. My husband had "come across" one day, just to see us for a few hours. He bombarded me with stories of the hardship and danger in West Beirut in order to convince me that I was better off where I was. The children, hostages in this struggle between their parents over their good—for I wished to throw off from them as well as myself the baggage of privilege—were themselves eager to return. They had exhausted the novelty of the physical freedom that the hills offered and in any case, like all the children of this country, suffered the anxiety that made them want always to be in touch with mother or father. While we pursued the argument, we heard that the Israelis had closed the crossing point between East and West Beirut.

For a few days, my husband shared our exile and became more sympathetic to my position. We had heard, after a day or two, that one crossing point was open but only to those with special permission. Our efforts to get permission were frustrated; only doctors were allowed back, or people with Red Cross cards, or diplomats. Even those, we heard, were told by Israeli soldiers at the barricade: "Why do you want to go there? You'll only die."

A day or two later all the crossings were open again. At this point, there were three places where one could get from East to West Beirut. The first was the road by the port, which was reserved for diplomats, Red Cross workers, and doctors, who were allowed to cross by car; the Israelis submitting everyone, even diplomats, to a search, confiscating food. The second crossing went by the National Museum. This was closed to cars; people had to carry their belongings and walk across. The third was at Galerie Simaan. This was by far the most dangerous crossing point but was the only one the general public could drive through. The problem was that the Israelis opened and closed the barricades at whim, announcing schedules that were not always followed.

We drove to the Galerie Simaan area after profusely thanking our hosts for their hospitality. They were reluctant to let us go. It was clear to them, as indeed it was to us, that the war was far from over and that we were heading for certain danger. When we arrived at the Dar el Sayyad circle in Hazmieh, we saw a huge line of cars waiting to be allowed across. The extraordinary thing was that, in spite of everything, there were far more people returning to West Beirut than trying to flee it. Perhaps they too felt the discomfort and pain of exile to be worse than the discomfort and danger of war.

We waited for two hours in the hot sun, before we finally turned away. We parked the car in our host's garage, where it was to stay for some weeks. My husband went to the museum and crossed over by foot. The next morning I took a taxi with the children to the museum, and we carried our bags across the border, watched by the Israelis on their tanks, to find my husband waiting with a taxi about a hundred yards away.

At last I had come home to Ras Beirut, then in its darkest hours. The siege of Beirut had begun. There was to be no water, no electricity, no food, or fuel for weeks. In those days of the siege, Beirut was an extraordinary place. Mahmoud Darwish, the Palestinian poet, has called it "a holy city," and so I think it was, the suffering and the spirit of the place sanctifying its struggle for survival.

The streets were strewn with rubbish; collection had stopped long ago. There were smoldering piles of garbage, and the air was thick with stench and smoke and the unpleasant humidity of summer. Unwashed people smelled of perspiration. The men were mostly unshaven. The previously dyed white showed through the uncared-for hair of women who had always been impeccably groomed. Children pitifully played their war games in the open streets. Refugee women humorously and courageously coped with their impossible situation, walking down the streets with plastic jugs of precious water from the wells balanced on one hip, infants on the other. Yet I felt, amazingly, a kind of euphoria inexplicable but for the parallel sense of apocalyptic doom hanging over the city.

Everything receded in those days except the feeling that we were the defending *us* versus a violating *them*. Anyone in West Beirut was *us*: fighters, refugees, foreign correspondents, rich, poor, Christians, Muslims, Lebanese, Palestinians, men, women, old, young, policemen—and, for all I know, murderers and thieves—we were all in it together and we felt a kind of closeness, a kind of unity that in normal times would have been unthinkable. We exchanged greetings and odd morsels of news with people we had never seen before and never would see again.

I had a sense of timelessness, as though the siege had always been and would always be; as though I had known no other reality. There was no work and no play, no proper time for doing this or that, for sleep or waking. We slept when we could; we woke when we had to. The structure of time collapsed, and hours fell about us like stones off a broken building. Sundays, Mondays—all the days of the week were alike and lost their character, and all the dates of the month as well.

Until this point, perhaps, the war that began in 1975 had never been clear, had never been pure; now, in the confrontation I felt something akin to a sublimely clear revelation of our role. Our familiar human selves were pitted against *them*, and *they* had become totally inhuman. Out of the muddy waters of the last seven years had emerged the true evil: Israel had presented itself thus at last, in open, undisguised, unpardonable ferocity. All of my previous hesitancy evaporated: Here was no doubt at all. This was the one battle in which I felt I could unquestioningly takes sides. All the criticisms that I had of the PLO's conduct in Lebanon—and there were many—receded, for it fought directly and gallantly, against the overwhelming force of the Israelis. Such courage as I possessed, such imagination, such idealism, such historical sense were all mobilized, focused on the necessity of resistance, which became to me the most meaningful political act of my life.

But how could I offer resistance to that overwhelming force? Not for a minute did I contemplate joining any army. It was too late to volunteer assistance to the hospitals: I had tried and been told that no one had the time to train me. My resistance was simply being there, looking after my family, and saying no to the leaflets. Perhaps what I did was foolish, a mere empty gesture that did no one any good. Yet to me it was not empty and, clearly, to many thousands of other people who had chosen the same course of action, it was not either.

There is an Arabic word that has been used a great deal in Lebanon in recent years but never so much as in those days: *assoumoud*. There is no single English sound-and-sense equivalent that I know of; rather it would have to be rendered by tapping the thesaurus's rich repository—*tenacity, steadfastness, resolution, endurance, indomitability*—all these words together, with their overlapping shades of meaning, give a sense of that noble word, *assoumoud*.

That it should have been used so often and so self-consciously by so many people points, I think, not only to what they thought of themselves but to the reality of the situation. No one, I think, in those weeks of the siege had the least illusion that there was even the remotest possibility of defeating the Israelis. This was the extraordinary thing: that the resistance was utterly hopeless, and that yet it took place.

In the beginning of the Battle of Beirut, there was division and considerable anger directed at the PLO. There were those who, pointing to the hopelessness of the situation, accused the PLO of inexcusable cynicism in subjecting the city to the cruelty of a borrowed doom. Whenever anyone in the PLO ventured to claim that Beirut would become the Arab Stalingrad or Hanoi—and speeches to that effect were regrettably frequent—native Beirutis responded furiously. Beirut, one heard all the time, was not a Palestinian city. "If you want a Hanoi or a Stalingrad, have it in your own cities, not in ours. This is not," Beirutis would angrily say, "your father's house—*beit abukum*." But as the Israeli attacks increased in ferocity and brutality, and as it became less clear that the Israelis were only after the PLO and not Beirut itself, as more people died and more buildings collapsed, there was a steady diminishing of such criticism. People increasingly identified with the fighters holding off the Israelis. A Lebanese woman acquaintance, who had for years been extremely critical of the PLO presence in Lebanon, said to me, on August 5, the day after a ferocious Israeli attack, in which they had attempted to enter the city and had been repulsed: "Weren't they magnificent? Bravo for the boys—*ashabab*! By God, *Wallah*, Bravo!"

What was daily life like in those days of siege? Fresh produce could not be had for love or money, but there were stocks of dried and canned foods and, when even these ran low, the many restaurants in the area, I found out later, added their private stocks to the supply. The most serious problem was the lack of water and fuel. What water was available was shared. Some buildings in Beirut—by then ours was one of them—were equipped simultaneously with artesian wells and generators, and these became the major source of survival for hundreds of thousands of lives. At first we ran the generator several hours a day, but later, when the fuel supply ended, we ran it just long enough, an hour or so a day, to pump the water.

An ancillary effect of a generator for pumping water was the luxury of a functional refrigerator, a rare blessing in those times. Of course, a refrigerator does not run very well on an hour or two of weak electricity a day in the hot summer, but it was enough to produce for visiting friends, amid gleeful cheers, a glass of beer or water that was hardly cold but better than tepid.

Queues formed wherever the motors were running and the water being pumped; long winding queues of men, women, and children patiently standing in line carrying a colorful assortment of blue, green, orange, red, yellow plastic containers. This artesian well water was not good for drinking, but many people drank it anyway. As the siege went on and the supply of butane gas ran out, people could not even boil it—the refugees who had no stoves could not boil it in any case. The major problem with the well water, however, was that it was salty. As the supply of safe drinking water in West Beirut ended, we began to hear of babies dying because of the consumption of salt. That was when many women, including the wife of the prime minister, began a sit-in at the American University to protest the inhumanity of the Israeli siege.

I would go out every morning (whenever I could, that is) to see my mother, to assure her, as the telephones were mostly moribund, that we were still alive and to make sure that she was too. A quick cup of coffee in her kitchen, her stock of drinking water standing in plastic bottles on the counter; a quick discussion with her house guests, bombed out of their own flat; a quick exchange of news; and then I would rush down the stairs again to scrounge some food from what was left at the grocery stores, the only shops open for months. I tried to make lentils, pasta, and rice palatable without tomatoes, garlic, or butter. My kitchen had long since run out of everything but dried food and some herbs and spices.

Housewives like me were for once almost totally liberated from the drudgery of daily chores. I mention pedestrian details like these both in stubborn loyalty to these days and to offset any tinge of romanticism that might linger around their memory: For, even in apocalypse you have to wash children's clothes; to think of ways to flush the toilet; to eat and drink and smoke. I never bothered to make the beds or to change the sheets; water was far more necessary for washing clothing. Cooking was reduced to a quick boil of the pasta and the sprinking on of the herbs. The fumes and soot from all the fires burning made it impossible to keep things clean. Anyway, one did not care. In that state of heightened feeling—with our world burning, shaking, dying—who cared about unmade beds, dirty floors, dusty tables? And yet I also remember every now and then going into a frenzy of housecleaning, but this had less to do with normal housewifely motives than with a kind of manic desire to clean up the whole world, the whole cruel world, the world of killing and of babies dying from drinking salty water and of horizons sooty with fire and pain.

The children played Monopoly and Scrabble. They quarreled; they often fell asleep on the floor. They discussed politics. They watched the Israeli ships, when it was quiet, and gave them "the finger" through the binoculars, unchided for their rudeness. From the balcony, they took snapshots of the battles in the distance, thinking to capture them on film but ending up with pictures of smoke. Once, having gone out on my daily excursion, I got caught in an air raid. When at last I could, I rushed home, trembling in anger at myself for having left the children alone; my husband and I usually alternated our departures from the house so that one of us would always be with them. I found them sitting in the "safe" room, reviewing geometry problems that had put one of them off during the year.

Still, for all of us, in those long hours between dashes to the shelter, boredom was a major threat. No one could concentrate long enough to read. I found myself scarcely able to get through a page or two at a time, but when I read at all it was only Jane Austen I could bear, finding, I suppose, some kind of comfort in that settled, remote, orderly world of hers. I read of gentlemen riding their horses up graveled drives when they came to call; ladies sipping their tea and discussing the latest lapse in decorum; young heroines being cut by snobbish dowagers; plump matrons having fits of the vapors; lovers being at last united after symmetrical rounds of misunderstanding—a world of refined language and sound structure. Structure: that more than anything, I suppose, I craved—an impregnable structure to be cherished in my world where reinforced concrete was collapsing all around me.

People sat together visiting. Those were the days for friendships. Mere acquaintances became bosom friends. Lips normally sealed in discreet silence whispered secrets that would never have been pried loose in normal times. Old friends became—how shall I put it?—closer than anyone can imagine: They became necessary, vital to each other's existence.

So many buildings had collapsed in the bombings, and so many people had been buried alive under them, that one of the great problems we faced was where to take shelter. The underground garages that had sufficed for an artillery war no longer offered even the illusion of safety. On the contrary, we felt threatened during the air raids by the very structures that had earlier protected us. Yet we could not stay in our flat, except in those moments when a weary fatalism overtook us, because of the danger of artillery fire. In addition, we had those prowling ships to contend with. Since they were always moving, calculating which walls to put between ourselves and death became impossible.

We compromised by taking shelter on the second floor of our building. The lawyer whose offices we used for this purpose lived on the other side of town and so had not come in for weeks. Thoughtfully, he had left his keys with us, and so, on the worst days, we would sit in the elegant reception room, surrounded by legal documents and other trappings of a civilized life, which served, under the circumstances, to remind us with a mocking irony of the gulf that lay between us and the normal, functioning world.

Around this time a rumor circulated that the Pope was coming to suffer with the city in order to bring about an end to the suffering. The idea, to use the vulgar phrase, blew my mind. At last! Something grand, noble, pure! A gesture, yes, but what meaning attached to it, what grandeur! But no. The rumors fizzled. Everyone laughed at me for having believed them in the first place. "Don't be silly," I was told. "It is too dangerous here for the Pope and it would be too compromising for him. There is, after all, a delicate international situation and the Vatican is, after all, part of the international establishment. Don't be silly." One friend of mine looked at me searchingly and said; "Did you really believe it? I can't believe that you really believed it."

One day I saw a Kurdish woman whom I regularly met on

the street. Normally we would greet each other cheerfully, and she would always break into a great smile, two solid-gold teeth gleaming. Today she looked depressed, worried. "What's the matter?" I asked. Her brother-in-law and two of his children had been killed in an air raid the day before, she told me, but that was not the worst thing. The worst thing was that the shelling was so bad they couldn't get to a cemetery and had had to throw the bodies into the sea. "What could we do?" she said. "Everyone is having to do this."

A crematorium that had once fallen into disrepair for lack of use was functioning at the American University of Beirut hospital, but it certainly could not cope with the huge number of dead. I do not know where people were buried during those days or how many were thrown into the sea. I know that until she told me this the problem had not crossed my mind, and I instantly blocked it out as too unbearable to contemplate.

We had on a regular basis what came to be called *gharat wahmieh*—mock air raids. Planes would come screaming overhead so suddenly and so loudly that our breath would be taken away. They would dive low, so low that we felt sure the end had come. Then, as suddenly as they came, the planes went without dropping a single bomb. Was this a form of psychological warfare? A cruel joke? A game? A declaration of air superiority—monopoly, rather? Practice? I do not know, but if it was possible for the Israelis to inspire further hatred, they did it with this device.

Through it all, there survived here and there fragments of that lengendary Beirut insouciance. One day, emerging from the supermarket with my cache of pasta, I came across SK. For a moment I did not know why her appearance startled me, and then it clicked. "S," I said in amazement, "you look as if you've just had your hair done." "I have." She laughed triumphantly, bringing her head close so that I could smell the hair spray. A hairdresser had set up a modest supply of water, had hooked up to a generator, and was shampooing, blow-drying, dyeing:

business as usual. And so, on this street at least, there was a small but steady stream of smart-looking women to offset the picture of total ruin.

On another occasion, a quiet day, my husband, restless, suggested that we go out for a walk. "Don't be silly," I said at first, so strange did it seem that we should go strolling at a time like this. Soon, however, we were on our way, walking through the AUB campus. In the beginning I was very tense. The open spaces were extremely threatening. It had become second nature to walk close to walls and to keep one eye out for possible shelter. But soon the beauty of the seaside campus, the tall cypress trees, the flowering hibiscus and oleander, the ivy-covered buildings, and the palm trees calmed my spirit and recalled normal times and other realities.

We walked and eventually found ourselves near the T's house." Shall we go in?" "Let's."

Although he was engaged in urgent University business, his wife was in the garden where we joined her. For an instant I thought I was hallucinating, but soon I was laughing in delight. There on the lawn she had set up a table on which was spread afternoon tea. There was a teapot with a crocheted tea cosy, the kind you buy at church bazaars; there were porcelain teacups, silver sugar tongs and teaspoons, embroidered linen napkins, and a little silver dish with biscuits. Both she and her sister, whose house had become uninhabitable because of the bombings, were wearing long, fashionable cotton kaftans. They were neatly groomed and freshly lipsticked. She was sitting, when we entered, with her legs elegantly crossed, one hand holding up her cup, the other fondling her dog, who knelt by her side. She looked, as she sipped her tea, as though she had never heard of war.

"I can't believe this," I said. "I feel as if I'm dreaming. How do you do it?"

"My dear, I would go mad if I didn't. We do this every afternoon at five unless it is physically impossible. Why don't you join us?" Clearly disbelief was still on my face, because she went on: "What do you want me to do? Die? When I must, I will. Meanwhile, every afternoon I have my tea." "But the ships..." I pointed out toward the sea where the gray monsters lay perfectly visible. The clear view of them from her open garden had, before I caught her gallant spirit, shaken me. "Oh well, when things are bad we don't do this, of course." She waved the whole thing away as it if were a minor detail.

"Tell me," she asked, as she poured tea for us, "what news of your mother?" And so, sipping tea I found myself drawn into the occasion, and we sat and chatted, and eventually left that mad tea party with renewed strength.

Eventually, exhaustion filtered insidiously through the stoicism. I remember the haggard look on every face, the circles under the eyes, the weight everyone lost. We were living among the dead and the dying, never knowing when we would be called to join their ranks, and so we took on the look of the dead. Sleep, as I've already said, was snatched at irregular intervals, and it was a restless, fitful sleep at that. There were all those stairs to climb, the elevators useless now, in modern, high-rise buildings, stripped of their efficiency—they were liabilities, burdens, really. Modernity and technology were now exclusively represented in the weapons; every other aspect of life was reduced to primitive, forgotten habits. The death machines worked; hardly anything else did. I remember raw, wordless fear, actual terror, gnawing at the bravest people, weakening them. And watching the children: my young son taking my hand and placing it over his pounding heart to show me; his thirteen-year-old brother sitting very still, very quietly, but very close to me, whispering on August 4, "Mummy, we're going to die today; for sure, we're going to die."

Those were the cataclysmic days, August 1, 4, and 12, on the first two of which the Israeli army tried unsuccessfully to enter West Beirut. Those were the worst days and the best, the most frightful, but the proudest, for they could not come in.

On Sunday, August 1, the Israeli attack began at around 4:00 in the morning and went on with savage intensity until a ceasefire was announced at 5:30 in the afternoon. The next day, relatively quiet, my husband and I decided to get our eldest son, scheduled to go to school abroad, out of Beirut together along with my aging mother, who was less and less able to cope with the physical strain of running up and down stairs.

We found a travel agent who was making arrangements to get people to and from just about every city in the world. We booked son and mother on a flight from Damascus, but the difficulty was getting them out of Beirut. That journey was supposed to take place on Wednesday, August 4, but by 1:00 A.M. it was clear that no one was going anywhere, as another ferocious battle was underway.

On Thursday, August 5, my husband went to the AUB to see what he could find out about convoys leaving West Beirut. He came rushing back with the announcement that one was being organized just then. We hurriedly got everything together and, with tearful, quiet hugs, said goodbye to my son and my mother as we saw them leave the American University hospital garage, part of a ten-car convoy. An hour later they had returned. The roads were unsafe; sniping was reported at the Galerie Simaan crossing. Both of them were literally shaking from what they had seen on their abortive journey. Buildings were still on fire; familiar streets were unrecognizable from the bombings. Tears had dried on both their dusty faces, but we were relieved that they were still alive.

The next day at eight in the morning, another convoy left, and they with it. They promised that somehow they would get word to us that they had arrived, but we knew that they might not be able to. At one-thirty, five and a half hours after they left, we got a phone call from Daora at the other end of Beirut, from the travel agent's office where they were supposed to rendezvous with the taxi to Damascus. They had not arrived. I collapsed into a chair by the telephone, utterly convinced that they were dead. My husband and I sat, staring out at the sea, not exchanging a single word. There was no way to find out what had happened to them. We were totally helpless.

As we sat there, there was a sudden scream of jets. It lasted just a few minutes: screaming, diving, *boom!*; black smoke and silence. We had jumped up at the first sound and called our younger boys together, but as quiet returned we resumed our posts by the telephone.

Outwardly perfectly calm, my husband reached for the radio and turned it on, tuning mechanically to the news. There had been a meeting we heard, conducted by Abu Ammar (Yasir Arafat) in an eight-story building in Sanayeh, housing two or three hundred refugees. The Israelis had just bombed the building, though Abu Ammar had left it safely a few minutes before. A new kind of weapon had been used—a vaccuum bomb, they said. Nothing was left of the building or the people in it.

I wept. My God, my God. What kind of people were the Israelis? For the first time in my life I knew pure, naked hate. At that moment, I think I could have killed. At that moment, I understood murder and war and the black heart of revenge.

The phone rang. My mother, unable to get through to us, had called the neighbors and they were transmitting the message. They had arrived safely, at long last, in Daora. It had taken them six-and-a-half hours to get there, a drive normally accomplished in fifteen or twenty minutes. Relief was accompanied by a sensation of total draining. My husband looked at me and said quietly, "You are taking the boys and leaving on Sunday." His brother, having to travel in order to keep his business alive, had made arrangements to leave that day. This time I neither quarreled nor argued. I was too tired. Besides, a detail was nagging at me that I had not revealed to my husband:

There were only two bottles of drinking water left in the kitchen.

Before I left my home that Sunday morning I walked through it, looking carefully at every room. Would this be the last time I saw it? Would my husband survive? I thought of all those people who had left Palestine a generation before. Would the Israelis take Beirut? Would they let people come back? I was neither sad nor resigned as I left. Everything had become empty and meaningless. The euphoria of the last weeks had worn off, had disintegrated like the city around me. The endless violence, death, and destruction; the never-ending wail of ambulance sirens; the interminable pattern of the talks at Baabda, punctuated at regular intervals by air raids and artillery fire; the reduction of life to scrounging for survival; the stream of new refugees as home after home was destroyed and section after section of the city fell; the babble of speculation about the future of the PLO, the future of Lebanon—all of it was like a horrible dream, a horrible mixture of hallucinatory images.

We left with a convoy of cars from the AUB hospital garage at 7:30 in the morning. My husband sat by the driver of the lead car; they would go only as far as the border of West Beirut, which at the time was marked by the ruined church of Mar Mikhail in Shayah. We wound our way through the city guided by the leader, experienced at this task. Since the beginning of the war in 1975, this man had made it possible for people to go to and from one spot or another in Beirut and, indeed, in Lebanon. Which roads were mined, which were plagued by snipers, which were safe—that was his job to know, although how he did it I cannot imagine.*

---

*On May 23, 1985, this brave and good man, Haj Omar Faour, was killed while shuttling nurses from the AUB hospital to their homes on the other side of the city. In tribute, the doctors, nurses, and orderlies of the hospital, wearing their white coats, walked silently in the funeral procession through the streets of Beirut.

Since the siege began we had not been out of our little quarter, Ras Beirut, by far the safest part of West Beirut. Now, as we drove through the city, through the streets and alleys, we tried to identify places and would gasp as we recognized a familiar landmark through the devastation and the smoke. We were not the first people in history to see our city in a ruined shambles, and I suppose we will not be the last, but it is an experience of infinite sadness. Even places that one had previously disliked, architecture, perhaps, that in normal times had offended one, took on in their recently martyred state a kind of transfigured, smoky beauty.

Arriving at the church, the head car stopped and parked aside, waving us on. We sped across the dividing line, up the five-hundred-meter stretch of road that was the no-man's-land between the church and the circle of Hazmieh. The boys turned to get a last, wistful glimpse at their father, who waved at them from the dusty car.

We spent four fearful days at my brother-in-law's house in Mansourieh, in the hills right above Beirut. We were once again in Israeli-held territory, and the shells, aimed at Beirut, flew over our heads. We watched their tanks lumber up and down the Aley road across the valley, as they went to and from their missions. From the hills we had once again a bird's-eye view of the city and of the battles still in progress. At night we could see the flares lighting this or that part of the dark city, as fires burned and phosphorus glowed.

It was from here that I witnessed the last day, the grand climax of the invasion. On Thursday, August 12, the air raids started around 6:00 A.M. and went on unabated until almost 6:00 P.M. I stood on the balcony and watched in disbelief, as wave after wave of bombing continued. It was as though the Israelis had gone stark, raving mad; as though they had achieved a paroxysm of violent hatred; a lunatic, destructive urge to kill, to blot out every living thing, to leave nothing standing, to eradicate the city. No military purpose was served that day: The long negotiations had come to an end satisfactory to the Israelis and an agreement on the evacuation of the PLO had been reached and announced. Standing there watching, I felt I could see all the tragic, cruel history of humanity concentrated: all the wars, the inquisitions, the persecutions, the wickedness, crimes great and small, genocides and individual murders, hatred, injustice, vengeance, domination, evil in all its forms, unleashed again in those endless hours of bombing.

The Prime Minister of Lebanon, Shafiq at Wazzan, appeared on television. Normally he was tiresomely diplomatic and longwinded, but this time he exploded: "What more do they want? We've done what they've asked. The PLO has agreed to all the terms. Agreement has been hard to come by, but we have achieved it. What do they want? There is only one thing left and that is for them to kill us all. Let them kill us all. We can do no more. Let the Americans face their responsibilities. Enough, enough. *Kafa, kafa*. We can do no more. *Kafa, kafa*." There was no pleading in his voice, no sadness, only a bottomless anger. He spat out the words, his face contorted in rage, his hands waving as though to send the words out faster. He was no longer just Prime Minister: He was Beirut, defiant, angry, proud, unbending. He had walked out of the latest meetings and was going home to sit, as all Beirut sat, and wait for the Israelis to do their worst. There was nothing else to be done.

I left Lebanon the next day with my children. We drove north to Tripoli, across the Syrian border to Homs, and on to Damascus. From there we flew to England and my sister's house, where I left my two younger boys and flew on to the United States to meet my eldest and to settle him down in his new school. Having done that, I returned to England and waited for my husband to join us there.

It was on English and American television that I saw the departure of the PLO fighters and, finally, Yasir Arafat himself from Beirut. All the miscalculations and mistakes of the last years, the heroism and valor of the last months were brought to fruition in that departure. The crowds that lined the streets, the families of the departing men who knew they might never see them again, the Lebanese public figures giving Arafat an official sendoff—surely everyone felt that both the PLO and Beirut would be impoverished by their divorce. The presence of the PLO had been a major factor in keeping Beirut's window open to the world and to the currents of modern history. Now that the question of what would become of the PLO and of Beirut was moot, there were tears and cheers; despair and hope, relief and anxiety mingled in the air.

Having assured himself that the war was really over after the arrival of the multinational forces, my husband joined us in England for a brief holiday. We hardly had time to enjoy it, however. He arrived on Saturday. On Tuesday we heard that the newly elected president of Lebanon, Bashir Gemayel, had been assassinated and on Wednesday morning that the Israelis had moved into West Beirut. For us in England the question was not whether to return, but how and whether we could. With all the press coverage of events in Beirut, the details we were most interested in were left out. Were the roads open? Could one get from Damascus to Beirut? Could one get from East to West Beirut? Even the Lebanese Embassy could not answer these questions, so we decided to get to Damascus and then hope for the best.

We flew to Damascus and then took a taxi to the border. There we changed cars and drove to Shtaura, in the Bekaa Valley. It was a lonely and dangerous drive. The marks of the Israeli air raids a few days earlier were everywhere to be seen, and there were no other cars on the road. In Shtaura we changed cars yet again; our new driver had no idea whether we could get to Beirut but he was willing to give it a try. The drive through Falougha, Mtein, and Dhour al Schweire was idyllic; the September air sweet with the smell of pines, as clear and crisp as autumn always is in the mountains of Lebanon. It was only later that we found out that our uneventful drive had been acutely dangerous, that several people had been killed on that lonely road in recent days.

There were, as it turned out, no barriers to West Beirut and we drove straight home, but entering the city under the circumstances was a melancholy and dispiriting experience. Proud, resistant Beirut had fallen at last. Israeli tanks stood on the severely damaged Boulevard Saeb Salam. It was only after the principal body of fighters had left and after the inexplicable departure of the multinational forces that the Israelis had entered the city. Even then, they had faced resistance, but, shorn now of their military backbone, the remaining fighters could do little.

Just before leaving London I had called my sister from Heathrow, where, owing to bad weather, we had been delayed for several hours, totally cut off from the news. "Have you heard?" she asked quietly. "It seems there's been a massacre in Beirut. There are no details yet, but reporters have been to the refugee camps and have seen hundreds of bodies." When we arrived in Damascus, the news was confirmed, although it was still rather vague.

Now, in Beirut, the full horror of the events in Sabra and Shatila was being revealed. People here responded to the massacre with revulsion and sadness, but with nothing like the shock that it elicited elsewhere. The saturation point had long since been passed, saturation with the never-ending suffering. A friend told me of her fatigue, which she had found well reflected in the words of a French newspaper: "*Les Libanais n'ont plus de larmes.*" "The Lebanese have no more tears." Read for *Lebanese* everyone in Lebanon, Palestinian as well as Lebanese, foreigners—everyone who has lived through what we have lived through in this wretched land.

Although an official inquiry was immediately announced, hardly anyone here was surprised, though many were angry, that it was to be conducted in secret. That the authorities felt it

better not to open the Pandora's box of inquiries, for accusation would follow accusation and bitterness would multiply
bitterness, and the wound would only deepen seemed to be a
satisfactory explanation. Yet there were those who felt strongly
that should an inquiry not be held and the wounds of all the
years not washed and dressed—should blame not be publicly
apportioned, punishment not meted out, and guilt not atoned
for—the wound would fester and its poison lead to even more
suffering. For years the thorny question of whether a general
amnesty should eventually be offered had been shunted aside
as too difficult. The very fine line between acts of war and
crimes had become, over the years, a broad span. Although in
the situation at hand the crimes were unquestionably clear,
they would inevitably raise others more difficult.

In any case, neither moral nor legal arguments could be
provided that weighed more heavily than the practical, political one: Leave it alone; enough is enough; don't rock the
already very unstable boat; nobody is innocent; everyone is
guilty; if we were to judge everyone, the whole country would
become a prison; who is to judge and who be judged when all
are guilty? Besides, is not general conciliation better than
recrimination and punishment? We are all so tired, better to
forget. And so, in these murky waters, murder had followed
murder and massacre had followed retaliatory massacre, and
everyone thought that each would be the last but it wasn't. To
this day the unasked question—Who was responsible and
should they be punished?—haunts the country.

The Israelis too conducted an inquiry and out of the
horror of Sabra and Shatila snatched a bogus moral victory.
The Kahane Commission was regarded here almost universally
as a fraud, which is not to say that its mere existence did not
cast shame on the thundering silence here. The fraud was
perceived because this crime was given such prominence while
all the others were forgotten. Sabra and Shatila were spoken of,
both in the Kahane report and in the Western press in general

as an aberration, as an event that marred the humanistic, moral record of Israel. An article in *Newsweek* dated October 4, titled "The Troubled Soul of Israel," overflowed with such phrases as *struggle for its soul, light unto nations, moral shock, human values, vision, redemption, just society, moral vision, moral point of view, ebbing spirit, pastoral, humane, democratic, sensitive, values, righteous*, and so on. (I can't help but note here that in the same article the sentences in which the word *Arabs* appears are tainted with *lurking, hating, stoking the fires, threatened to consume, hatred, dirtiest manual labor, terrorists, less than human, cheap Arab labor*, etc.) This just, decent "light unto the nations" was not the Israel we knew, but the creation of precisely such verbal chicanery. Still, from the glass house of silence, it was difficult for anyone here to cast stones at the false structure of a moral Israel.

And the world reacted violently. The Israelis, having done what they wanted to do in Beirut—having taken the arms, the people, and the books (several libraries and archives were raided) they wanted—withdrew in disgrace. Already they had experienced Beirut. One day during the occupation my husband and I were walking on Hamra, having accomplished a necessary errand, for in those days most people stayed at home as much as possible. There, in one of the cafés, sat a couple of Israeli officers. The waiter bringing their coffee was visibly miserable, the picture of sullen, frowning reluctance. The very next day, an Israeli officer was shot in another café. After that, the soldiers were no longer seen except in their purely military persona: Guns at the ready, they walked and drove in groups, wary and distant.

Stories had begun to emerge of the spies in our midst. Beirut, we found out, had been riddled with them. Every neighborhood, street, organization, militia, and party had been penetrated. There was a man who lived on the street not far from my home. We had taken him at face value as the lunatic he seemed to be. Apparently obsessed with feathers, he had been dubbed *Abu 'l Rish* ("Father of Feathers"). He had constructed a strange, movable hut of rags and feathers, and he wore a very peculiar, pointed hat over his pointed, bearded face. He would dart out into the street and ring a brass bell at the passing cars. Many are those who, moved by his madness and homelessness, gave him money in charity, and who later beat their fists on their foreheads in anger when they read that in reality he had been a captain in the Israeli army.

After the Israelis left, we began to hear of the most extraordinary aspect of the occupation. Arrests, harassments, shootings, even the obligatory looting: These were what everyone expected, and indeed, they had occurred. But the thing that no one expected was what we, on hearing about it for the first time, greeted with hesitant laughs. Gradually, we discovered that what had seemed like a single incident had become, in fact, a trademark and taken on far more serious dimensions.

The Israeli soldiers, wherever they had been, had defecated in choice places. On books, furniture, clothes, and carpets; on bedroom floors; near toilet seats and in bathtubs; on school desks; and in shop windows, people found the rotting feces. Someone swore she knew of one house near the airport where the distraught housewife had discovered feces in her washing machine and dishwasher. One man, we heard, went to his office and saw on every single desk except his own the offensive, stinking pile. Triumphantly, he sat at his desk and gloated over his unhappy colleagues. Then he opened his drawer, and there, neatly lying among the files, was his bequest from the Israeli army.

And so, after all the ruin and tragedy, after the destruction and pain, the dead and the dying, the lacerated bodies and blinded eyes, the burned and disfigured faces, the widows and orphans—after all this there was left only a great heap of excrement. The fires had died, snuffed out in a mound of dung. A ghastly joke, symbol of an overriding contempt, a cosmic stink had become the memorial to those months of agony.

VI

Ghosts:
A Meditation
on the
Massacres

T he shop window is boarded up now, but through the cracks between the planks you can catch a glimpse of the dark interior, which couldn't be more than four or five meters wide and long. On the otherwise bare floor, amid balls of dust, lie yellow scraps of old newspapers, a piece of patterned material that must once have been part of a dress, a battered old tin bowl, a broken stool lying upside down, and a plastic baby bottle with its rubber nipple half torn off and hanging to one side. There is nothing else here but the remains of an old sign outside the shop, hanging precariously from one end.

Before the war the sign advertised the presence of a pâtisserie. It was never very good, and the small cakes on the display shelves always seemed to be dried up and old, the creamy icings a decidedly suspicious color. In 1975, at the beginning of the war, the cakes stopped coming, and to no one's regret, the place closed down. Through the protective iron grate and the cracked glass window, one could see that the refrigerators and display cases had been removed. The shop was thoroughly empty but for the remnants strewn around: dozens of paper cake shells, stained cardboard dishes, paper napkins and cups, strings of flat cardboard ice cream spoons, and what was left of an old chair.

Thus the place remained for several years. Once as I walked by, I saw a rat in the far corner and, once, a kitten that had somehow gotten in and was now trapped, mewing pathetically for help that never came nor ever could, for it was too frightened or weak to come to the grate. Later I saw it lying dead, its tiny carcass rotting and covered with crawling things.

In the summer of 1982, the place suddenly came alive. The iron grate lay, twisted and broken, on the sidewalk, mingled with what was left of the glass window and the wooden frame. Inside, several women were bustling around, bumping into each other as they swept and washed down the floor. Some of them, in various stages of pregnancy, must have been younger than they looked. A din was created by the large number of small barefoot children. Some toddled around clutching their mothers' skirts. Others, a little older, assisted in the work, but more often than not got in the way, their efforts rewarded with good-natured smacks and loud imprecations.

Soon they had settled down in their new place of refuge. They were, I discovered, wives and children of men in Al Fateh, the largest Palestinian resistance group. They had left their homes in the refugee camps and had been brought here to the relative safety of Ras Beirut. Every morning, the men would drive up, their jeep roaring to a stop in front of the shop. They would jump out, bringing bread and water and other provisions. The children would clamber about their fathers, hanging on to necks and arms, as husbands and wives exchanged loud conversation over the communal clatter. Sometimes the men would linger; squatting on the floor, they would gulp down some food, or sit leaning against a wall, unshaved, heads nodding occasionally in exhaustion, as the women plied them with questions. Most often, however, they would no sooner roar in than they would jump back in their jeep and roar off again, leaving the women and children watching them from the sidewalk, shouting a last word at their receding figures.

As I passed the shop on my daily forage for food and news during the long and bitter weeks of the siege, I wondered how these women managed. The room boasted no bathroom or water supply of any sort, but somehow they had converted it into kitchen, sleeping place, and delivery room—for at least two babies were born here. A dilapidated Primus stove was set up during the cooking on the pavement outside. A single, large tin utensil served as saucepan and dish and doubled, on other occasions, as laundry bowl and bathtub. Mats were laid out inside, and one could always see a child or woman stretched out asleep. Mothers of young babies would squat indoors or out, nursing their infants; toddlers would run around bare bottomed, while one of the women would hang out the laundry on a line manufactured from discarded wire and hung between a streetlight and a telephone pole.

I was tempted once or twice to stop and converse with the women, to offer neighborly help, but somehow I never did, although we always exchanged greetings. The strange thing was that, in spite of their appalling situation, they seemed totally self-sufficient. I felt that offers of help would have been proudly, even humorously, declined, and that it was *they* who offered *me* something—a reality, a kind of substantialness that I lacked—for they were what the war was all about. There was a normal, everyday sort of cheerfulness among them that astonished me. Instead of grimness and bitterness, there was an endless stream of chatter and banter, as they scolded a wayward child or separated two small wrestling cousins, or bustled in and out of that wretched room or took a leisurely stroll around the block when it was safe to do so, scarves demurely wrapped around their heads and knotted under their chins, arms swinging energetically for all the world as if it were a holiday picnic.

When I left Beirut in mid-August, they were still there. When I returned in mid-September, the shop was empty, boarded up as it is now. The PLO fighters had left the city. The Israeli army patrolled the empty streets.

Where did they go, my erstwhile neighbors? To Sabra? To Shatila?

☐

In my living room, right next to the piano, is my broken record player. It's not totally broken: The cover keeps falling apart, and the needle is worn, but it still goes. I know I should get a new one, but I haven't the heart to throw this old machine away, for every time I look at it I remember him.

We had bought the set in 1962. It had remained in perfect condition until it was smashed by artillery. We had been about to throw the whole thing out when I thought that perhaps he could salvage some parts and make use of them. He came and took it away, laughing at my thought, but obliged anyway. A few weeks later he turned up on our doorstep with a triumphant grin on his face, and a patched-together stereo set in his arms.

Many is the time we ran to his little shop just off Hamra, looked through the window to see him perched on his high stool, tinkering with a radio or telephone or lamp. We would bring him home, *SOS*, to fix a recalcitrant television set or vacuum cleaner. Rarely would he pronounce the death sentence on anything mechanical, and it was only when he did that we would give up on it. He did us favors as well, helping us with our Christmas shopping, for instance, advising us on what brand of radio or cassette recorder to buy for our boys, and going with us to ensure a discount.

He was a perfectly ordinary-looking man. Short and pudgy, he had a soft, kind voice and white skin. His wire-rimmed glasses would move up his nose as it crinkled when he made a joke, often not a very funny one. We would laugh partly to spare his feelings and partly because of a deep-rooted sympathy with that ordinariness that made it hard to tell a good joke. He seemed a born bachelor and we would often tease him about his single state, threatening to find him a bride. Good-naturedly, he would fall in with our mood, pointing to his balding head as proof of his ineligibility as a prospective bridegroom. He used to holiday regularly in Rumania, which was cheaper than the other, more conventional tourist spots, and bring us back dull little tales about his mild adventures there, his tone always full of wonder about a life so different from his own, for he had never, I think, been anywhere else outside Lebanon.

One day we heard, to our astonishment, that he had at last married, and that he and his wife had had a child. We didn't see much of him after that. He preferred to stay in his village, eschewing the noise, the uncertainty, the danger, the cruelty of Beirut.

His village was Bhamdoun. In 1983, his body lay on the ground, rotting and stinking in the sun amid the crumbled stone ruins of the town—his body and his wife's and his baby's, among about three hundred others.

☐

Today, Damour is no more. Weeds grow where the town once flourished.

In the old days, before the war, we used to drive through Damour just about every Sunday. Sometimes we would be on our way to Sidon or Tyre, taking visitors to those cities, or just going ourselves to see what the latest digs had uncovered, stopping to eat fresh fish on the way. Sometimes we would drive to Damour on the coastal highway and then, from the heart of the town, we would take the steep road up, up into the green mountains of the Shouf to the lovely town of Deir el Kamar and, across the valley, to Beit ed Dine, where Lamartine visited the Emir Bashir in his splendid but rough palace, with its graceful wood- and stonework, its lovely ceilings and windows, its baths and fountains cool amid the dark cypress trees. Sometimes we would drive down to Damour after having lunched in Shimlan, our heads heavy with the *araq* we had drunk with the barbecued lamb and chicken, the *hummos* and *tabbouli*; chasing bees away while we ate and drank amid the clatter and bustle of the Cliff House, pausing now and then to admire the magnificent view.

Sometimes we would drive to Damour just for the pleasure of seeing it. On one side of the road, its houses spread into the foothills and provided a sense of space and graciousness. They were made of handhewn stone in the lovely old architecture, with high elegant arches topped by slanting red roofs. The wooden slatted shutters that framed the pointed windows were most often painted green but were sometimes white or blue. On the other side of the road and all the way to the sea lay the rich fields, the pride of Damour. The jeweled citrus groves sparkled in the sun, oranges and lemons gleaming as the farmers in straw hats stretched out their hands to pluck them. The fields of lettuce were sumptuous velvet carpets of deep green, and the banana groves were a brighter green, with yellow fruit stabbing the broad leaves. Beyond the fields, on to the horizon, the blue waters of the Mediterranean glistened, turning a turbulent, frothy gray-green during the winter storms.

Along the road on either side stood wooden stalls covered with mats of jute sacking or, sometimes, concrete or tin roofs, under which stood the farmers' wives selling fruit and vegetables. We used to buy oranges, grapefruits, sweet and bitter lemons, bananas, and lettuce from these stalls, but there were also crates full of potatoes, cabbage, cauliflower, zucchini, eggplants, beans, and tomatoes. On the way back to Beirut we would stop in Na'meh where, in front of the sand-colored church, we would buy radishes, as well as parsley, mint, and green onions for *tabbouli* from the boys who stood at the roadside waving at the passing cars, one hand holding up a red bunch, the other a green one, as they called the prices.

Under the idyllic beauty of Damour, however, lay a violent reality. The guns were growing in number and, with them, hatred.

It was in January 1976 that Damour was sacked. Many of its inhabitants were killed, their bodies lying on the ground, arms and legs outstretched, eyes staring. Those who were not killed escaped by boat and took refuge at first in monasteries and convents in the mountains. The town was looted, and the houses picked clean, stripped not only of furniture but of shutters, doors, tiles, faucets—everything—then burned. When it was over, they looked like so many pock-marked death's-heads. In the battle most of the fields were burned as well. The glitter was gone and all that was left was black devastation.

I looked carefully at the ghastly pictures in the paper, trying to recognize some of the faces of the dead, hoping that I wouldn't. Our favorite stall had been run by a rather shy woman with red cheeks that dimpled generously as she smiled. When we first knew her, she was surrounded by several small children, and as our stops at her stall were repeated we never could recognize the changing faces. Finally one day we asked her how many children she had. Eleven, she answered proudly. We had respondingly pronounced the obligatory "*Ism Allah,*" invoking the name of God in protective benediction; and she had dimpled away, her latest offspring on her hip as she added the last orange to the bag on the scales.

If I didn't recognize her picture in that horrible portrait gallery, it was not necessarily because it wasn't there, but rather because the pictures of the dead do not resemble the living.

□

As one crosses the new and shining bridge, over the Beirut River, one's eye is caught by a small glass box standing on the pavement of the side overlooking the city. In the box is a plaster statue of the Virgin Mary and her Child. At their feet lie plastic flowers, pinks and blues and whites matching the dress worn by the Holy Mother. The veil that covers her head and body is royal blue, piped with gold thread. Her face is blank; whatever suggestion of sanctity there is in the roadside altar with its white tallow candles is brought by the worshiper's faith, not by any artistic effect. There is a long tradition of these boxes: Anyone who has traveled in Lebanon knows them well. They suddenly appear on the mountain roads, just before a nasty curve, the pastel shades clothing the saints striking against the rich brownish-red soil, the strong greens of the pine trees, and the gray rocks.

This particular boxed Virgin and Child presides over the area known as Karantina, which was once the quarantine station attached to the nearby Beirut harbor. Karantina was once alive with thousands of people who lived in ramshackle houses behind a great stone wall. Today, however, if one were to follow the frozen stare of the Virgin, one would look at the other side of the bridge and beyond to see only clumps of grass, a few rocks, a kind of blank landscape matching the emptiness of the holy gaze.

It was here in January 1976 that the first massacre took place. It was followed by the flight of a panic-stricken remnant and the bulldozing of the houses. The night was cold. The men were young and hooded. Hundreds of people were shot.

Bodies were mutilated. Women screamed. Ancient couples pleaded in vain with boys young enough to be their grandsons, but cruel enough to kill, to destroy, to burn, to pursue the aged.

There is a well-known photograph of that night. In the background a fire is consuming the pathetic homes of this slum community; the television antennas are faintly visible through the smoke. A man wearing a white *kaffiyeh* is running, holding two barefoot little boys by the hand. A small boy running behind him has his hands raised in surrender. Two girls are fleeing in front of them, their feet bare on the hard earth, their heads turned toward the fire.

The focus of the picture is a middle-aged woman, white scarf wound around her head, her face distorted in agony, this moment no doubt the climax of her hard and miserable life. Her hands are stretched out, palms open toward the sky in the immemorial gesture of pleading. Because her head is leaning desperately to one side, one is reminded, as if by a distant echo, of a Pieta shorn of its beauty and serenity. The young man to whom she is appealing is standing with automatic rifle pointing to that same remorseless sky. He is the picture of masculine power. He seems tall, with strong shoulders slightly stooping as though ready to strike her. His long legs are bent in motion, one booted foot raised a little off the ground, the other firmly planted on it. One has the sense that his boot is ready to trample on all the humanity around, his own included.

His head is covered by what seems to be a rough woolen sack, his face hidden by this inhuman mask. You can't even guess at his expression. Is he tortured, sad, agonizing about the pain he is causing? Or is he angry, still furiously mourning comrades fallen before this final victory? Is there a look of insane pleasure on that covered face? Or a calculating grimness; a sense that this must be done, however hateful?

Why, indeed, is he wearing a mask? From whom is he hiding? What recognition is he avoiding?

☐

When the Karantina massacre took place, rumors were rife that the young men who had committed it were high on drugs. Perhaps they were. The point is, we couldn't believe such cruelty to be naturally possible. Believing them on cocaine left our humanity intact. *Father forgive them, for they know not what they do*.

But such an explanation is harder to believe today.

Too often, too many people have done too many unspeakable things. They are not from one district or one community or one class or one religion. They are among us all; it seems, *from* us all. They seem to have been driven not by cocaine—at least not by cocaine alone—but by that infinitely more potent drug of pure hatred, hatred and revenge.

What does it mean, then? What do all these acts of unimaginable cruelty mean?

I do not raise the question with any philosophical intent, for this is not a question of philosophy for me. I have lived these things, and I want to know what they mean. I want to know whether I can escape the apparently inescapable conclusion that it is in the nature of the beast, that any of us could do it, that *I* could do it. Could I, if pushed far enough, yet do it?

I have not seen my baby's body mangled in the dust or my fiancée's raped body lying bloody in the street, legs wide apart and eyes blank. I have not seen my father dishonored in death or my mother's nakedness exposed to the world. I have not seen my beautiful, strong, young husband reduced to unidentifiable bits of flesh. I have not seen my life's labor blown up in a brilliant second by a foolish boy with a stick of dynamite; nor have I stood in front of the rubble that was my home, knowing it to be beyond salvation. I have not had any of the experiences that have become part of daily life in this tortured land. And since I haven't, I no longer dare say that I would not do such cruel things as have been done.

Besides, is there a difference between killing people by pressing a button as you soar through the sky and killing people while you see terror on their faces? Is there a difference between the man who stands on a distant hill, taking aim through a telescopic lens and firing at a city—holding his ears as the missiles burst out of the gun, checking to see if the shells have hit the target, remaining clean; and, if he has no imagination, not seeing the burned and broken bodies, the blood spurting and the limbs flying, not hearing the tinkle of falling glass and the thunder of collapsing concrete or the screams of terror and sobs of grief—is there a difference between this man and the man who kills with his own hand, seeing, smelling, hearing the result of his own deed even as it is accomplished? What is the difference? Why do people find one act of war more acceptable than another? Is there difference for the victim or for the culprit—or is the difference only in the spectator's reaction? Is it because we say to ourselves, with such smug assurance, "I could never do that," and dissociate ourselves utterly from the deed, feeling relieved at our own unblemished humanity?

It is easy here in Beirut to look at every passing stranger and see the face of a potential murderer. Those throat-cutters, those who rose in the dark of the night, who put their pitiless hands around the necks of women and infants and cut them, who are they? Which ones?

Yet it is when I look at my own face in the mirror that I am most frightened. Is mine the face of one of the damned?

VII

Remnants

*S*pring, *1989*: I sit, scribbling, at the same desk, looking out the same window at the same blue waters that blend on the horizon with the same blue sky, yet around me, everything has changed. In the beginning, I had a sense that history was in the making and that I was a witness to it. There was a certain excitement in that position, a kind of exuberance at living an important moment and trying to cast an oblique light on it by recording how people—ordinary, everyday people—react, how they live during such momentous events.

There is a roar in the sky. Another military plane screams by. I do not look at it, as a kind of snub, I suppose. I'd rather watch the flock of pigeons circling over the building in front of me, white and black flashes in the sky as they circle mindlessly, rather like us, repeating every day what we did yesterday, in ever narrower circles. History seems stuck here, like an old needle stuck in the groove of an old record. After the great convulsion of the Israeli invasion we thought, for better or worse, that we would at least have an end to war. But, no—it began again, as hideous, as bloody, as numbing as ever. And again and again it begins and ends, and then begins again. Each time more people die, more people leave.

Over the years, what started as a worrisome question has become a major obsession as, we look around us at our steadily diminishing numbers. Should we go or stay? Who is the next person of our acquaintance giving up the struggle, packing up and leaving? "Are you planning to go?" The question haunts us all, and we ask it constantly of our friends, always afraid to hear the affirmative answer, relieved at the negative. There is another, related question never far from our consciousness: In staying, are we working against history, fighting fruitlessly against the inevitable, or will we prove to have done useful work after all, like the salmon who spawn and produce new life after their inexplicable and exhausting struggle against the river's current?

Those who left made sense. "This place is hopeless," they said. "The war is going to go on forever. There is no possible solution. Remember the Hundred Years War?" they mumbled, or, more modestly, the Thirty Years War? Off they went, and after each goodbye our hearts sank a little bit more and our depression deepened, but we stayed. In the beginning, people left for a few weeks, a few months. They took suitcases and a few valuables. Today, more permanent moves are being made, yet few are those who have not left behind a flat or a house to return to in the event that peace is finally restored. For some people, of course, there never was a choice: Economics or the lack of the right papers dictated their staying. But those of us who chose to stay cannot help but realize that, with every new departure, the task becomes more difficult and the gamble riskier. The stakes are our lives.

From the beginning, there has been a peculiar keeping of accounts of who was here for what and who went away when and why and for how long. This account-keeping becomes particularly feverish—bitter, almost or perhaps I should say, triumphant—after the most intense episodes of violence. It is at the most frightening times that being alone is most painful. One feels a terror that one has bet on the wrong number, and then, when the moment passes, a sense of triumph that one saw it through.

What does it mean, then, to have stayed? What have we hoped to accomplish? First of all, I think, we have reclaimed and redefined our humanity. We did not do merely what we were told; we did not obey the obvious command to leave, or to be divided. We were more stubborn than those who bombed and killed and burned. In the end we proved stronger, tougher than they. Where they sought division, we insisted on community. Where they wanted a monochromatic existence, we carried a palette of colors that we defiantly splashed around everywhere we went. Where they sowed death, we reaped life. We refused their arguments, and we proved that life can spit at death.

We have tried to clean our own streets until the garbage overwhelmed us. We have tried to march for peace, succeeding in the early days of the war to express ourselves thus, failing later as the forces against which we were to march proved so massive and ruthless as to make our protests irrelevant. We have demanded the release of the kidnapped, and been ignored. Our only triumph is our stubborn persistence, our active refusal to fall into the partitionist, exclusivist camps, our carrying on the normal life of society, preserving it, our readiness to take over again when the war ends.

Our children still go to school; there are still schools to go to. If their standards have declined—and who can argue that they have not?—the most intelligent students still get accepted at the best universities abroad and pursue their studies. When we get ill, there are still doctors to attend to us. There are still merchants to provide us with what we need, entertainers to make us laugh, and artists to express our pain. Life has continued and continues still.

Those who are outside looking in see only the war. For us, there are people, friends, life, activity, production, commitments, a profound intensity of meaning. It is these things that have given us the strength to continue, even when we are filled with doubt, for they reassert themselves during and after every battle.

Most important of all, there has been a sense of community so powerful as to compensate for the difficulties of life. I have felt, over the years, in spite of the depression, the fear, and the doubts, a sense of privilege at having shared this impossible fragment of history with so many good people. We have looked evil in the face; we have spoken to wicked men; we have asked ourselves the questions that most people are spared; and we have understood that the lines between goodness and evil are sometimes broad and clear, sometimes thin and invisible. We have done these things together.

We have understood our own and each other's limitations in a way that has made us all more tolerant of humanity. There are, for instance, no more illusions left in any of us about bravery and stoicism, about who can stand how much and for how long. We have seen each other crack under the pressure of events, each one in his own way, each one at his own time and for his own reason; we have seen each other lose dignity, seen each other shake in humiliating fear. We used to laugh at these weaknesses but no longer do so. We have seen ourselves and each other under a microscope for years, naked blobs of humanity on glass slides scrutinized through the merciless lens of history, and nothing any of us does surprises the rest anymore.

We understand and accept our own and our friends' limitations.

We have paid a heavy price for this community. Let those who would comment lightly on us beware: We are unforgiving judges of those who have not shared our experiences. We are like a secret society. We have our own language; we recognize signs that no one else does; we joke about our most intense pain, bewildering outsiders; we walk a tightrope pitched over an abyss of panic that a novice does not even perceive, let alone understand. We are provoked to anger and fear by the smallest detail while suffering calamity calmly. We are, each of us, bundles of nerves wound up so tightly into little balls of extra-awareness that we bounce off the walls of our personal and collective catastrophes with an apparent ease. Every new battle, every new death, every new car bombing and massacre, every new piece of bad news is felt by each of us as a personal injury to be borne silently. A patient in hospital being subjected to an endless series of injections, jabs, and other ignominies, will eventually cease to protest and will lapse into quiet endurance, even as each jab is felt by every nerve in his body.

So, at all costs, we doggedly, stubbornly carry on, but always with an obsessive eye on the outside world against whose established reality we measure our own, fraught with doubt.

Today, the Beiruti's eye is constantly confronted by buildings in various stages of collapse; broken glass and torn awnings; dangling and broken electric signs that once glittered in advertising gaudiness; shabby, dirty, overcrowded streets; blocks full of refugees, their children playing in the piles of rubbish scattered here and there, monuments to the war; telephone and electric lines hanging loosely from bent poles; stray dogs and cats, diseased and slow, sniffing at the garbage on empty corners. Ancient ruins are, somehow, beautiful and uplifting; the imagination works on them, restores them to their original state and function and brings those who built them to life. Modern ruins, however, are ugly and depressing. It is not the imagination but the memory that works on them, and there is nothing sweet in the memory of war.

The ear, too, is constantly affronted not only with explosions, bullets, screaming jets, and sirens, but also with the sound of glass shattering (or, later, the so-familiar sound of glass being swept up), of the anarchic traffic negotiating ever narrower streets and smaller neighborhoods. Now, the most recent irritant is the sound of an ever-increasing number of intensely noisy generators lining the streets or perched high up on balconies, making a deafening roar. When and if it ever comes, peace will mean to us quiet as much as anything else.

Our horizons have been so narrowed by the war that we suffer a terrible form of claustrophobia and, every now and then, remind ourselves of the old days when we would drive for hours to get somewhere far away. We used to drive south to Tyre for the day or north to Tripoli, east to Baalbeck, or even on to Damascus; up mountains, down valleys, and across plains. We used to go up to the Cedars and walk in their ancient shade or to Beiteddin to enjoy the palace; we used to picnic in the woods and by the waterfalls; follow a creek by foot and pose for pictures by a Roman aqueduct. We used to wander around the old port at Byblos and then eat fish freshly caught from the sea if we felt like it. On Sundays we would often visit friends who had a house in the mountains and sip tea by the roses while the children played under the trees.

Now we are confined, not only each to our own city and town but even to our own quarter in the city. The confinement is not only physical but social as well. I look in my telephone book sometimes and read it to remind myself of the existence of people whom I have forgotten, to see if there isn't someone around whom I can visit as a change from my few remaining friends. My friends' words, motions, and gestures are so predictable that I can anticipate them, and often I feel I may as well talk to myself (which, by the way, I have caught myself doing once or twice). But the telephone book yields nothing but a profound depression. I read the names of those who have moved away, gone to America, England, Amman, or Athens; those who have died, some naturally, some violently; and those whom I no longer care to see. I have shed people in rather the same way as I have shed clothes that no longer fit, or whose shape no longer appeals to me, and put them away. In a strangely morbid way, however, when the old telephone book is worn out and tattered and I start a new one, I mechanically copy into it all the names and numbers, including those of the distant and the dead, as though by this doubtful magic I would resuscitate them and the old days, as though I would erase the last terrible years.

Crushed and pulled and pushed from all sides, we have a tendency today to retreat into our own houses. If there is a reigning symbol of the war, it must be the refugee, and those of us who have not—yet—lost our homes cling to them, self-consciously hanging on to what we recognize as the most elementary of human requirements. Obsessively, we clean and decorate our houses. We have made of our interiors little, self-sufficient worlds, insulated as much as possible from the ravages outside. But no matter how hard we try, we cannot shut out the war, even at moments of relative quiet. We are locked into the situation, penetrated by it. We carry it in us and around with us. We have developed strange habits and nervous tics; we are a living catalogue of psychosomatic symptoms.

Probably the single most dominant feeling now—greater by far than the latent sense of triumph at having survived, greater than sadness and fear, greater even than their closest rival, an immense and overriding fatigue—is the feeling of terrible waste and the anger which accompanies it. One of my dearest friends was shot and killed at a barricade three years ago. I feel her senseless death everyday, a fresh raw wound, the pain almost as intense as it was on the first day, when I thought I should burst, and when I knew at last what they meant when they spoke of a broken heart.

It is not only the waste of human life that one deplores, although that more than anything. A beautiful old house—or even an ugly new one—is destroyed and a city is diminished. A shop is blown up, even a shabby one owned by a greedy and less than scrupulous merchant—does it not represent years of labor? Trees are cut or burned down; forests are destroyed. Whole villages, towns, and portions of cities have been leveled; churches and mosques have been gutted; schools and hospitals wrecked; factories have collapsed. Time has been wasted; years have passed; loneliness and emptiness have encroached. I have had my youth ushered into middle age by war. My children's— all the children's—childhood was lived in its shadow. My youngest son was four when the war began; now he is in university.

A whole generation has grown up in this war, and as I look about me, I feel confident that the torch we have struggled to keep lit has been successfully passed to them. There are those who will disagree with me on this, who see confessionalism and fanaticism permeating the youth here. Certainly this is true, but only in a minority. The vast majority are as receptive as ever to the old ideals, and impatient with the narrow thinking which they wave off as a legacy of the war. Many of them have grown up isolated from each other's regions and cultures, but most are brave and good and honest enough to take the risks involved in renewing the trust. As parents—and as teachers—we tried, over the years, to instill in them a knowledge of that aspect of nature that they had not much opportunity to study as they grew up; to impress on them the existence of such things as goodness, beauty, kindness, and justice, and they have been excellent students of this lesson.

Loneliness and emptiness have encroached. When the

war began, my mother and two of my sisters lived here. Another sister and my brother used to visit regularly, and I had cousins, uncles, aunts. Today, I am alone, the last of my family in Beirut. Of my husband's large family, only his sister and one or two cousins remain. The others have all gone away. They rarely write or call. Of course, the mail doesn't work well and neither do the telephones, but perhaps the real reason is that they want to forget, to blot Beirut out of their memories.

But, still and again, in the quiet times life goes on. Very early every morning, a woman in the building across the street from me lets down a plastic bag from her fourth floor apartment, uncoiling the string slowly to control the bag's descent. The concierge, waiting, watches the bag come down, unfastens it, and takes from it small parcels wrapped in tin foil, which he then sets out on the sidewalk. All the stray cats of the neighborhood, who have for some time been pacing the empty streets, meowing expectantly, approach the food, bristling at one another occasionally—though unnecessarily, for there is plenty to go around—and they eat to their hearts' content. Then they lie in the sun, or disappear for the rest of the day. I have been watching this silent little morning ritual for years, throughout the war. I watched it this morning, as the sunrise clouds turned from a flaming red to a gaudy pink and then finally dissolved away altogether. I have found comfort in the gratuitous kindness, the unspoken generosity of the thing, in its stubborn regularity, its unmitigated continuity. Even in periods of fighting, as soon as the shells and bullets stop flying, the plastic bag makes its inexorable descent, and the cats eat.

When they can, young people go out to dinner, to night-clubs, and beaches as they do everywhere. They laugh and dance, ski and swim. Plays and concerts are produced, dinners given and attended. The latest styles are still in the boutiques and the latest technologies available in the shops.

I do not think much about the outcome anymore, preferring to live in the moment, enjoying what I can with whomever I can. Today we had lunch with newly made friends. The meal was served in their garden. It is springtime and the weather was splendid, the sun shining and warm, the sky a deep, dark blue, the spring flowers in full bloom. Tonight we will visit old friends who have just returned, temporarily, from abroad. We will take our happiness in small doses, lingering over it, feeling it, savoring the joy.

April 13, 1989: Today, as everyone knows, is the fourteenth anniversary of the beginning of the war. I say that everyone knows because everyone is talking about it. Many of the past anniversaries went by unnoticed. The reason today's is remembered is that the war is on again, full blast. As I write, I can hear Grad missiles being fired a few hundred meters away, and I can see the smoke and dust generated by their takeoff. What a sound they make: first a crash, then a deep, grating sound, a rumble, and then a shrill scream. My windows rattle. In the distance, a few seconds later, I hear the thud of their arrival. Soon, I suppose, I shall hear the whistle and crash of the shells landing here in response. The few cars on the street outside race by, beeping continuously in panic. This round of hostilities has caused the deaths of many people caught in their cars. On the first day, when the shelling took everyone by surprise after more than two years of relative peace, it began at 7:30 in the morning, during rush hour traffic. People were on their way to work or taking their children to school. The toll that day was fifty-three dead. When yesterday's shelling began suddenly, some drivers abandoned their cars and ran for cover.

We slept in our beds last night, fully dressed, ready to go downstairs when necessary. But the shelling did not begin until 5:30 this morning—at least I think not. We may have slept through it this time, as we did one night last week, sedated by the *araq* we had drunk earlier on, torpid with fatigue after so many sleepless nights.

I am trying very hard right now not to think of my husband, Samir, who has gone to Bir Hassan near the airport. He had some work to do there, and I did not try to stop him. Current wisdom says that you never tell anyone, not even your husband, what to do—never influence another's decision, never take the slightest responsibility for another's fate. It is impossible to anticipate which road or room or even chair is to be the fatal one.

This morning, after the initial fright, it was quiet for a while and I went out to do some errands. The street was utterly deserted, and I noticed the barber next door had piled sandbags in front of his glass door. We had asked him to arrange sandbags for our garage, to separate our wretched corridor shelter from the cars and boilers. He obliged, and at this very moment, there is a truckful of sand in the garage and a couple of men filling the bags.

Samir returned from Bir Hassan. "*Ma fi shi*," he said about his dangerous trip. "There is nothing. Things seemed normal." But he arrived just in time, because very soon we had to go downstairs as the *whoosh* and crash of incoming artillery shells sent us scuttling. Unlike past years, however, there are not that many people in our shelter. Most of our neighbors have gone away. In January some of them had come back from abroad, hoping to stay, but the renewal of the war made them leave again.

How did this round of fighting begin? How do they all begin? A sparking incident, a few days of *hudu'hathir* ("cautious calm"), incendiary statements made on all sides, and then the explosion. Schools close, shops close. Foreign intervention on one side or another, or both; accusing statements from both sides. A larger, more terrible explosion, more intense bombardments. More incendiary statements. More bombings. Schools remain closed. The only shops open are the groceries. The municipality stops collecting garbage; the refuse piles on streetcorners become mountains, which eventually collapse into streams of torn plastic bags and rotting vegetables. Eventually, people start setting fire to the stinking mass, and then the air becomes smoky and the stink pervasive.

One ceasefire after another is announced and then broken. Religious leaders on all sides appeal for mercy on behalf of the civilian population; their appeals are ignored. Medical authorities appeal to all sides to spare hospitals and clinics from bombardment; their appeals are ignored. Ambassadors of great powers and small go in procession to visit leaders on all sides; they emerge from their meetings to be questioned by crowds of reporters hoping to extract from them a straw of hope, and their statements are all alike. Their countries are staunchly for peace in Lebanon; they feel profound sympathy for the people; they express profound sorrow for the dead and the wounded and for the loss and damage of property. In Rome, the Pope prays for peace. Emigrés in foreign capitals, waving little Lebanese flags, demonstrate for an end to the fighting. The bombings continue. More people leave the country. Power lines and pumping stations are hit, and electricity and water are rationed further. The war goes on.

For years we have been told that there are "red lines" in Lebanon drawn up by the international community. One of these coincides with the Green Line that divides the city. Neither side is, under any circumstances, permitted to cross it. Thus the demarcation lines have remained fixed almost since the beginning.

There are no red lines, however, to protect the people. It is quite permissible, it seems, to bomb the population on both sides while achieving no strategic advancement whatever. And this agreement is overseen by regional and world powers, both those who make a great issue of human rights and those who do not bother to disguise their brutality with hypocritical affectations of humanity.

April 14, 1989: Last night, they say, was one of the worst of the entire war, a fitting anniversary celebration. My anger knows no bounds.

The other night in the shelter we listened to Mozart on the radio between news flashes. When we came upstairs—there was still some electricity then—we watched a soccer match on TV: Brazil versus the rest of the world. Last night there was no Mozart and no electricity. We lit a few candles, standing them with difficulty on the uneven, bare, concrete floor of the shelter, and someone, a disembodied voice, remarked at how pretty the candlelight was. We were badly bitten by mosquitoes. As we slapped at them and scratched ourselves, someone said, "We are like rats. *Wallah*, by God, we are like rats down here."

Around 1:00 A.M., after a half hour of calm, we went upstairs, flashlights in hand, dragging the pillows and blankets that had not much helped alleviate the discomfort. No sooner had we arrived at home, than we heard another whistle and crash. This time I at last was adamant. "I'm not going down any more," I said to Samir. "That's it." It was not suicidal madness on my part or even philosophical fatalism. It was fatigue and a kind of angry defiance. "That's it," I said, "no more." I got into my bed but leaped up with every crashing shell. Finally—I have no idea at what time—I dozed off.

I woke up at 7:30. It was quiet outside. I showered and dressed, choosing my clothes carefully. I chose a dark blue skirt and a sweater and a white blouse, polished my black shoes, and fixed my hair. In patching up my appearance, in choosing particularly neat and orderly clothes, I felt I was undoing the humiliation of my ratlike state last night.

I visited everyone I could, saying *"Hamdillah 'alassalameh"* ("Praise God for your safety") to everyone.

April 17, 1989: Yesterday was pure hell. For the first time in all these years, I feel that I can't bear any more. Our judgment is failing, and our nerves utterly shattered.

In the afternoon it seemed quiet. Feeling restless, I decided to go out to visit the K's, not three hundred meters away. As I walked, the great gun down the street boomed. My heart leaped and I ran. But then, sipping coffee at my friends' house, I felt calm again. Samir called and said he was coming. A few minutes later we heard a whistle and a crash, followed by the sound of glass falling, a sure sign that the shell had landed close by. We froze, thinking of Samir on the street. For a few minutes we sat still, waiting. I looked out the window and saw L with her children, running towards her niece's house, where they have been sleeping. I called to her. She looked up and waved as she ran, not smiling. "Near us," I could hear her say, as she rushed on. Still no sign of Samir. At last the phone rang. "I am calling from someone's house," he said. "The brother here was good enough to let me in. I'll stay here for a while." "Are you all right?" "Yes, yes." He did not sound all right. Later he came, pale, and drank the coffee quickly made by N and then he said, "Let's go home."

Our walk home—our run, rather—was terrifying. The street was utterly deserted, and all the buildings lining it had their doors locked, their shutters down. There would be no place to take cover.

Later I had my private moment face-to-face with death. I had gone out to the balcony to make sure the bottles of butane gas were closed. As I bent over, turning the valve, I heard a shell whiz by. I froze. "This is it," I thought. The explosion and the sound of shrapnel tinkling as it landed had me still bent over, still frozen. By the time I left the balcony and started downstairs, I felt weak and quivery. I felt tears flowing, tears of anger and humiliation as well as fear.

In the shelter, we gasped at the news of the soccer disaster in England that killed ninety-five people. As the shells poured down around us, someone said wryly, "Thank your God that you are not watching soccer in England."

April 20, 1989: A whole day of calm yesterday. This morning I opened all the shutters, letting the spring sun into the house. The shutters have been down for weeks, although the many holes in them remind me that past experience has proved them incapable of keeping out shrapnel and bullets.

Mother called yesterday afternoon from Washington, D.C. She was in hysterics. "You have to get out of there," she sobbed. "I might never hear your voice again." I tried to calm her, laughing at her hysteria. "Don't worry," I said. "We've been through this hundreds of times before, and so have you." This is, of course, not true. With the exception of the summer of 1982, this is by far the worst confrontation we have ever seen. Also we are seven years older than in 1982 and worn out by all we have been through since. "And I've just been out and bought a strawberry *tarte*." "Don't talk to me of strawberry *tartes*," she almost shouted, infuriated by my attempt to inject banality into her vision of doom. "Promise me you'll leave immediately." "Okay, okay," I said to her, shaken, hushing her terror with a promise, which I have no intention of keeping, to make travel arrangements. Her vivid impression of our impending death was contagious, and by the time I hung up, I was deeply depressed.

April 23, 1989: It has been relatively quiet for a few days—a "truce," everyone is careful to say, not a ceasefire. But the great gun down the street has been booming regularly, directed, it seems, at the sea, part of the naval blockade. The gun has acquired a nickname in the neighborhood; everyone refers to it as "Abou Abdou,"* a wonderfully incongruous domestic touch implied by this name, whose origin I cannot explain but which is typical of the cynical humor of Beirutis.

---

*Abou Abdou: Father of Abdou. Abdou is a common name meaning "His (God's) servant." Many fighters here have taken as *nom de guerre* "Abou someone."

I went to bid S goodbye today. She has decided to take her children and join her husband who works abroad. We met at her niece's house. Her sisters were there to see her off as well. Everyone was depressed and tense. As we hugged each other wordlessly, I felt my tears coming and hers too, so I left quickly, before the taxi arrived that was to take them to Damascus. I have said goodbye to so many people over the years.

They are burning garbage on streetcorners all over the city. The alley near us is blocked by the garbage and swarming with rats and flies. The other day I saw a squashed rat near it, its guts spilled out on the asphalt amid rotting orange peels. There is a film of grime on every surface in the house, no matter how often I wipe it off, and on the horizon an ugly brown streak runs like a brushstroke from east to west, as far as I can see. The day the gasoline and storage tanks in Daora were exploded by artillery about three weeks ago—the explosion blew out windows miles away, and the entire area around Daora was devastated—there was a huge column of black smoke over the city. In the afternoon and the next day, it blotted out the sun entirely. For days, we sneezed and coughed and our eyes burned.

The water supply has been cut off for weeks. All we have now is bottled drinking water and that from our artesian well, which, undiluted with sweet water from the municipal pumps, is thoroughly brackish. Others have no water at all, and, as in past years, people come to our building carrying plastic containers that they fill from our well. Yesterday we passed a hose to the German church parish house behind us. It is full of people who, bombed out of their own homes, have taken refuge there. The parish house is blessed with a fully equipped, proper shelter.

Yesterday T came to take a shower. He hasn't a drop of water in his flat. No sooner did he start to bathe than Abou Abdou started booming. He emerged quickly and rushed away. "These are going out," I tried to reassure him, used to distinguishing the sounds. "Yes," he said, "but they might start responding any minute. Thanks." And off he went.

If the quiet continues tomorrow, I suppose I will be called to a meeting at the college. We haven't met for two weeks; the last time we met I had to run home while shells were crashing down. There is nothing to decide. The spring semester had just begun. All the schools and universities have been closed since mid-March. It is out of the question to resume classes before things settle down entirely, and who knows when that will be?

I went up there yesterday to look at the damage caused by the four shells that landed on campus. RN, the security chief, took me on a tour—he has done this so often, it seems, that he has a fixed route, and I joke with him about his being a guide of these modern ruins, reminding me of the men who used to show us around the Pyramids or the temples of Baalbek. The tour began with a look at what was left of the shells themselves, carefully locked up in the generator room near Irwin Hall. I wonder why we are keeping them and think that perhaps one day the sculpture students might turn them into works of art. The damage on campus could have been worse, I suppose, and no one was injured, thank God. Most of the glass on campus has been blown out; a corner of the Fine Arts Building where my office is, has been torn off, smashing our department secretary's office. The office typewriter is in pieces—they found it on the tennis court—and it is exhibited as a trophy, along with the computer terminal, which seems to be intact. Air conditioning and water pipes have been broken, electric wires cut, diesel storage tanks smashed. The "scene shop," a large outdoor shed recently constructed to store sets for the theater has been partially destroyed. It took years to get the funds to build the shed in the first place, and now we have to begin again. All our efforts over the years, it seems, have just kept us standing still.

I have a constant headache and have noticed recently that my right eye, which has taken on a will of its own, blinks repeatedly, even as I angrily try to stop it by pressing it hard. My smoking gets on my husband's nerves almost as much as his complaints about it get on mine. I have promised to stop smoking as soon as the war ends. "That's what you always say," he snaps. We are like a pair of snapping turtles these days: *snap, snap.* We are each other's outlets for the tension.

April 24, 1989: We went to see N, Samir's sister yesterday. She has not been out of her house for seven weeks. We teased her about her excessive caution, but her terror was contagious and we went home sooner than planned. In the afternoon, taking advantage of the continuing calm and the lovely spring weather, we went to visit the S's. We sat in their garden, which was in full bloom, not yet dried up by the lack of water. The windows of their villa were blown out last week, and they showed us where the shells landed. When we got up to leave, she cut some flowers for me: white roses, purple sweet peas, and yellow daises. On our way home, my husband exchanged warm greetings with someone I did not recognize and who turned out to be the man in whose house he took refuge the day he got caught in the shelling.

This morning, on my way back from my daily pilgrimage to the supermarket, I ran into a journalist friend. He confirmed my worst fears. Having interviewed everyone, he feels this calm is not going to last. We're bound for more shelling. The thought of it makes me sick. There hasn't been enough damage, he said, nor have there been enough casualties to move the international community to action. He laughed when I asked him whether we can expect mercy from any of the leaders, local or international, and didn't bother to answer the question—which sounded silly, even to me.

They have just announced on the news that a French ship carrying fuel oil has at last been allowed to dock and unload, so we will have two hours of electricity a day, beginning tomorrow.

April 25, 1989: Last night, after a calm evening, we blew out our candles around 11:30. Suddenly, at midnight, all hell broke loose. I don't know how we made it downstairs. We came up from the shelter at 5:00 A.M., cramped and exhausted.

April 27, 1989: In Tunis, there is an emergency meeting of foreign ministers of the Arab League to discuss the crisis here. Is it possible to hope that they might help engineer an end to the war? We hear that they are thinking of sending an Arab force to observe the ceasefire. That is good news, but our reaction stops short of elation as memories of past forces that came and went obtrude. In 1976 an Arab peacekeeping force, including troops from Syria, Saudi Arabia, Sudan, and Yemen came. They stayed about a year then left when the peace collapsed. Only the Syrian troops remained, and they left during the Israeli invasion of 1982. After the Israeli invasion, a multinational force composed of troops from the United States, France, Britain, and Italy came to oversee the evacuation of Palestinian forces. They left and then came back a few weeks later in the wake of the massacres in Sabra and Shatila. Then, after the U.S. and French headquarters were bombed, they left again, this time for good. In 1987, after months of street fighting between rival militias in West Beirut, Syrian forces arrived again to keep the peace. Then we had the terrible sieges and fights in the Palestinian refugee camps, the war between the Shiite militias, and now the shelling between the Lebanese and Syrian armies. In the meantime, after a major Israeli incursion in 1978, a United Nations force came to the south. It was composed of troops from Holland, Sweden, Norway, Ireland, Fiji, Nepal, Nigeria, Senegal, and probably others I have forgotten. But they have not prevented the Israeli incursions and air raids, let alone the great invasion of 1982, nor their continuing occupation of South Lebanon.

It is not easy to be optimistic about another force being sent here. The whole world has come and gone, it seems, and the war has continued.

Last night, suddenly, the electricity came and we cheered. Although we were only supposed to have two hours of power, someone, it seems, forgot to switch off our share. We are delighted, but our friends to whom we gleefully announce our good fortune are envious and indignant. The electricity has been on for thirteen hours now.

April 28, 1989: The water came this morning! I poured it on the plants. What a pleasure it was to fill the watering bucket over and over again and to soak the leaves, the soil; to see the geraniums lifting their drooping heads at last. I gave them shower after shower and felt intoxicated at the feel of my wet feet as the excess water splashed on the floor. Samir had the dreary task of filling the bottles and kettles.

Yesterday the Arab League foreign ministers declared that they had negotiated a ceasefire in Lebanon. A few hours later we went downstairs as the shells began to fall. The smell of cordite was heavy in the night air.

April 29, 1989: The ceasefire is tenuous. Abou Abdou has been regularly booming out, but so far today there has been no response from the other side. Still, in a mood of optimism as tenuous as the ceasefire, I brought up the sheets, pillows, and candles from the shelter.

It is extremely hot today, with a true *khamasin*, the hot, southwesterly wind from the desert, blowing fine sand at us, stifling, and a haze everywhere. I went out to test the collective pulse and found to my dismay that most of the shops are still closed and more sandbags are being piled up. PS was supervising the whitewashing of the cement blocks he has piled protectively around his supermarket—his bitter memories of the numerous times the place has been gutted are shared by all of us. "Trying to beautify it?" I asked. "It is really no use trying. Nothing can make those concrete blocks look better." PS only grinned at me in answer.

May 2, 1989: The observers have not come. None of the Arab countries, it seems, is eager to get involved in the Lebanese quagmire. Adou Abdou has been going off at regular intervals, night and day. We jump at every single shot, so terrible is the sound. At night, there is a great flash of white light before the boom. But except for a brief time a couple of days ago, the other side has not been answering.

We visited the K's, as we so often do these long and dreary afternoons. Suddenly, as we sipped our coffee, we heard a great commotion on the street and went out on to the balcony to see what was happening. A truck full of flour had arrived to deliver its load at the bakery, which has been closed for weeks because of the lack of flour and fuel. Masses of small boys were clambering all over the truck and its cargo, yelling gleefully as they helped the bakery workers, who were wearing protective sacks on their heads, unload the heavy bags. The joy of the boys cheered us up, and we laughed as we watched them darting about, actually impeding rather than assisting in the work of the men. However, the latter did not seem to mind in the least and appeared amused by the attention they were getting in the neighborhood. Many other people watched the show from their balconies and everyone had a good time.

In the morning I had gone up to the college to meet LG, the department secretary. I was to help her clean up the mess in her office, but by the time I arrived she had already done most of the work. One of the college janitors was sweeping up the glass, pulling out the pieces still hanging, jagged, from the twisted window frames. Green computer sheets of class lists, torn examination booklets, old telephone messages, course syllabi, mimeographed English grammar exercises—we went through them all to see what was salvageable and then consigned the rest to the garbage barrel, where they lay amid the broken glass and unidentifiable bits of rubble. By the time we finished, our hands were grimy, black, and sticky. As I left, I glanced back and saw her busily setting up a temporary space for herself in another office, arranging boxes of stationery, paper clips, and pencils in the drawers of her new desk; hanging a humorous poster of Garfield the cat bemoaning the necessity of dieting, which she had rescued from the rubble, and the College calendar, designed and executed by the art students. She will make her new corner as cheerful and efficient as the old one and will be ready to go back to work immediately.

After I left her, I wandered down to the corridor near the Dean's office, where I saw some colleagues for the first time since the fighting began. We hugged and kissed each other, with lots of "*hamdillah 'alassalameh's*" all around, and then we settled down to exchange the usual stories. EB told us, laughing, how he set up a primitive pulley system in his seventh floor apartment to help him bring up the containers of water that he has to collect from the neighborhood wells.

Everybody grumbles ceaselessly about the water and electricity, and many of my friends tell me urgently, "Put that in your book." They ask themselves if the world knows what a terrible problem this is. Then they sigh and say, "The world doesn't care if we die, let alone if we don't have water."

May 3, 1989: I was called up to a meeting at the college to discuss the possibility of resuming classes next week. We fixed a tentative date, knowing we probably would not make it. The meeting was desultory. We have no idea whether the ceasefire will hold, no idea how many teachers have left the country, or, for that matter, students and staff members. This will be the first time that we do not finish the academic year. Although all the years have seen disruption of the schools, we have always managed to finish the year.

May 4, 1989: Is it possible? At 2:15 we heard the news that the Arab League representative had spoken with all sides, and no more obstacles stand in the way of a permanent ceasefire.

We went out to visit my sister-in-law, who still hasn't left her home. The traffic jam on the way clearly expressed the new hope that people feel. When we got there, we found that she and her husband hadn't heard the news. She wasn't ready to believe it quite nor to undo the barricade of mattresses in the entrance to her apartment behind which she has been sleeping all these weeks.

May 5, 1989: Probably, she was right. The gun boomed in the evening, in the night, and in the morning. Our elation was shortlived indeed.

May 7, 1989: Yesterday was Id al Fitr, the holiday that ends the fast of Ramadan. We called all our Muslim friends to wish them happy holidays and promised we would visit them in the next couple of days, leaving the first day of the celebration to them and their families.

Samir went out for a walk in the afternoon and got back around 6:00 P.M. We were preparing to watch a videotape when, all of a sudden, there was a series of tremendous crashes. We leaped up, left everything, and ran down to the shelter, as the shells crashed down by the tens. I tried to take a moment to pull down the shutters at least, but Samir was shouting at me over the noise to leave everything. I caught a glimpse of a cloud of smoke coming from the direction of the AUB dormitories across the street.

In the shelter we saw the J's. Although she is normally a very composed woman, she was sitting in a heap, shaking and sobbing in her holiday attire. They had been making their holiday visits to the family when the shelling caught them on the street. When she at last recovered and was able to speak, she kept saying, over and over, "I don't know how we survived. I don't know how we made it."

We were in the shelter for six hours. None of us had even had time to think of bringing a flashlight or pillows. We sat on the bare floors in the dark for some time, but eventually Hassan, the concierge managed to scrounge up some chairs and candles.

May 9, 1989: It is now two days since I slept at all. The shelling has been almost continuous, and I should feel incoherent and dimwitted, but I don't. I feel I can see clearly today.

This is the future. Small wars, in which local leaders with local quarrels are backed by larger powers and they by the great powers. Individuals cease to exist. We are nothing—our lives, our homes, our personal problems, our ambitions, all nothing. There is a large scheme of things, which perhaps a handful of people in the world understand and manipulate. And there are the weapons.

The other day, the daily *Ad Diyar* had a whole page of pictures—and prices—of the weapons used in this round. Throughout the war, each new round of fighting has introduced us to new arms, new forms of killing devices. Our lesson progressed from the Kalashnikovs of early 1975 to the mounted recoilless rifles and the larger mortars and artillery, especially the 155mm, in 1976. Also, we learned of the Grad. In 1978 we heard of Stalin's Organ, the multibarreled rocket launcher that fires up to forty missiles at a time. (Yes, we too, laughed at the name and its erotic connotations.) Then we discovered the RPG (rocket-propelled grenade). In 1982, during the Israeli invasion, we were introduced to phosphorus and cluster bombs, as well as boobytrapped toys that blew children to bits when they picked them up. In 1984 we learned firsthand of the sixteen inch guns on the U.S.S. *New Jersey*.

The star of this year's show has been the 240mm mortar, whose shells can penetrate two reinforced concrete floors. This gun, we are told, is of World War II vintage, but its age doesn't seem to have made it less effective. Also, we have been learning how deadly anti-aircraft shells can be when they are fired horizontally, exploding in the air and sending their shrapnel to kill whoever happens to be passing. We are the guinea pigs on whom new weapons are being tried out and obsolete ones used up lest they go to waste.

The cost of these things is staggering. A single 240mm shell, according to the *Diyar*, cost $9,500. The 160mm shell costs $1,500, the 155mm $1,300, the 130mm $700, the 122mm $300, and so on down to the single Kalashnikov bullet, which costs 30 cents. The other night alone, they estimated that ten thousand shells had poured down over the city. If we take the middle cost of $1,500 per shell, that would mean $15 million in one night. And this war has been going on for fourteen years, not always with that intensity, true, but still, fourteen years. And ours is only one of the dozens of so-called small wars going on around the world. In fact, there is nothing small about them, except their victims.

Next to this simple reality, what do the ancient words mean: *freedom, humanity, decency, liberation, democracy, truth, civilization, culture?* Nothing. Like us, they mean nothing. Still, the factories must be kept busy, I suppose.

It is now 7:45 A.M. I came up from the shelter at 5:00, had my coffee, and bathed. Since it is still quiet, I shall go out for a brief walk. One never knows when the shelling will resume, but I must try to—I would have said, recover my dignity, my humanity, restate my free will—but those words sound hollow and silly. Again I have dressed with care: I have chosen dignified clothes and black patent leather pumps, instead of the jogging shoes and espadrilles of the shelter. Those clothes are the badge of my shame. I detest them and will throw them away one day or, better still, burn them. I have washed my hair and even put on some makeup. I look to myself like an over-painted stage actress, so unused have I become to seeing color on my lips. I know that I look almost as awful as I feel, but I must try.

On the way, I will buy some cigarettes, in spite of my husband, in spite of the doctors and the cancer associations. Also some batteries and candles. I never seem to have enough of those. And aspirin, plenty of aspirin.

May 11, 1989: The other night in the shelter I saw a cockroach. It was an enormous one, a member of a flying species that thrives here especially in the hot months. Often in the summer one of these creatures would fly in through the window and the whole household would be in pandemonium, so disgusting are they. Cushions, brooms, shoes, anything at hand would be held up in the general mobilization against this invidious intruder; and everyone would shudder when it was finally tracked down and crushed, its remains swept up and flushed down the toilet.

That night in the shelter I felt no such revulsion. I watched the cockroach crawling in the corner near which I sat and wished it no harm, feeling that it was a kindred spirit, a creature, like me, of dark hidden places, living out its life in ignominy. It seems that everyone down there reacted in similar fashion, for there was none of the flurry that normally accompanies a sighting of one of these beasts. When someone finally crushed it with his shoe, the crunching sound brought no reaction and the cadaver was merely kicked absentmindedly aside into the outer space of the garage, to be swept up later with the cigarette butts and other debris of our sojourn in the shelter.

It is now two weeks since the Arab League foreign ministers in Tunis called for a ceasefire, announcing they were sending an inter-Arab force of truce observers. The shelling has been worse than ever, and we have been downstairs for days at a time. The death toll has been rising daily, and the names of those killed and wounded are read over the radio.

Meanwhile, the great powers are expressing their concern, and the Pope has offered us his prayers.

May 15, 1989: It has been fairly quiet. I went up to the college this morning, where I saw many people, including some from the east side. Everyone has strange little stories to tell, mostly having to do with narrow escapes. DJ told a story that touched her so much that her eyes teared as she told it. A young man, a neighbor of hers, with several young daughters has been sleeping on the landing near her apartment with his brood during the shelling. After settling everyone down on mattresses and pillows, he sits up all night, smoking and drinking coffee to keep himself awake, lest one of the little girls should wake up in terror when a shell explodes nearby. It is only at dawn when his wife wakes up and he hands over the watch to her that he allows himself to sleep.

Another person told how the two elderly uncles with whom he lives these days quarrel over which radio station to listen to at news time. Neither tolerates the political views of the other, and each insists on turning on the radio station belonging to the party he supports. We laughed at this scene.

Everyone is expecting more shelling, so, having infected each other with that fear, we scattered and went home.

On my way home, I overheard a quarrel between a young husband and wife. She says, "But how do you know what is going to happen to us?" He answers gruffly, "Do *you* know what is going to happen? Whatever happens, this is our home, and we are staying in it." "But the children—" "The children: *Mitlon mitl ghairhun*" ("They will be like everyone else"). We're not going anywhere." "We can go and stay with my

parents in the village," she pleaded. "We're not going anywhere, and that's final." She is in tears by now, but he is
adamant.

Yesterday, R called from London. Hearing her voice and
remembering the calm and order of her life there filled me with
a terrible feeling of desolation, loneliness, almost panic.

May 16, 1989: When we heard the explosion, we thought at
first they had resumed shelling. But then we heard the ambulances and shooting, and we knew it was a bomb. I was invited
to lunch with D, and she was preparing the meal at the moment
of the blast. We immediately switched on the radio and very
soon there was a news flash. The explosion was in Aishe
Bakkar, that was all they knew at this point. A few minutes
later they said the Mufti (the religious head of the Sunnite
community) was passing at the time. The third flash said that
the Mufti had been taken to hospital, that the explosion was
huge and caused by a car bomb, that it had been placed near a
building in which our friends the K's lived, and that the building had collapsed. We gasped, thinking of our friends. A few
minutes later came the announcement that the Mufti was dead
and that many others had died as well.

We sat frozen, emotions running amok. Pain at the death
of the Mufti, terror at what this might mean to the situation,
deep anxiety about our friends, about all the others who might
be there, and, of course, the usual rage at this odious form of
murder. D's husband was late for lunch. She began to feel sure
that he might be in the area of the bombing. There were no
telephones and no way for her to find out whether he was safe.
I tried to calm her worries, although I shared them. More and
more flashes came over the radio. It wasn't until the evening
that the final toll was reported. Twenty-two people were
killed, more than a hundred and fifty wounded. Nothing
about the K's.

Finally D's husband turned up, as shaken as we were, but

pretending otherwise to calm us down. He had not been far from where the disaster had taken place and had had to take a long detour to get home as the area was sealed off by the police and the civil defense workers.

I went home and sat by the telephone. Everyone was deeply depressed about the assassination. All the friends of the K's wanted to know what had happened to them, but there was no way to find out. Some friends tried to get to their house but were turned away. It was no use calling the hospital, as it would be in pandemonium. We would simply have to wait.

May 19, 1989: The Islamic rites for the dead are deeply moving in their dignity and simplicity. We sat silently, all the women together, the men in another room in the mosque building, waiting for them to bring the body for prayers and burial. She was killed when the building collapsed, but the rest of the family miraculously survived, though all were injured. We had been to visit L in the hospital. Among her other injuries, she has been deafened, temporarily we hope. There were 150 kilograms of TNT in that bomb.

Every fifteen minutes or so, the sheik's voice would rise, chanting the Koranic verses for the dead. After each reading he would invite the faithful to recite the Fatiha and then, palms open upward, the Muslims would pray silently while the rest of us sat, heads bowed. Everyone wept, the pain of the loss weighing on us—after the months of pain, an unbearable burden. And the unfairness, the overwhelming unfairness of it! I thought constantly of my friend S, killed three years ago, and relived her death. I thought to myself as I listened to the Koran, that it was no wonder that people believed in a heaven and a hell, rewards and punishments enormous enough to contain such emotions as we were now feeling, as well as the hope that an omniscient being knew who was responsible for this and all the other anonymous crimes.

The mosque is in one of the most devastated parts of

Beirut, Aishe Bakkar, further destroyed by the car bomb. We saw the building that had collapsed as a result of the bomb, as well as the marks of the shelling of the last few weeks. As we left someone pointed out the ruins of the small house in which a whole family had been killed during the shelling, buried when their home came down over their heads.

There is a seven-day period of national mourning for the Mufti and a three-day general strike. At the time of his funeral, the church bells tolled all over the city, a gesture of profound significance and one that I found deeply moving. Also, and in the same spirit, the Maronite Patriarch opened his doors in Bkerke to receive condolences on the death of the Mufti for those who, like himself, would not be able to come to West Beirut and to Dar al Fatwa (the seat of the Sunnite community). When the television news at night showed the Patriarch, visibly saddened, accepting condolences, I was moved to tears. This is the true spirit of the place, not the mutilating voilence between the sects that has been going on for years.

This morning I saw a sight that lifted my spirits. As I walked by the German church near my house, I saw the blue blossoms of a jacaranda tree blending with the pink flowers on a nearby oleander bush, along with a scarlet hibiscus and a purple bougainvillea—all the blossoms surrounded by various shades of green. For a moment I forgot the ugly, rubbish-strewn street on which I walked and just stood and looked at the colors, transported. I looked up further and saw the architecture of some of the lovely old houses here. I have been so busy looking at the dirt on the ruined streets that I have not done justice to the remaining beauty on my daily path.

May 20, 1989: We are on tenterhooks, waiting for the Arab summit that is to take place in Casablanca in three days.

A few days ago, Lakhdar Ibrahimi, the representative of the Arab League, was shuttling between points in the capital to negotiate a final ceasefire. LK overheard this conversation between a mother and her small child. who did not want to go out. "They will start bombing us now," he cried, hoping to stay in the shelter. "No, no," soothed the mother. "Don't worry. *Ammo* ('Uncle') Ibrahimi is in Beirut. They won't bomb while he is here."

May 27, 1989: The Arab summit ended yesterday. N and K were with us as we listened to the final communiqué read over the radio. They got up to leave, saying, "They have let us down. There is nothing in this for us. Just words." We shall have to wait and see.

Abou Abdou boomed in the night.

May 30, 1989: We are waiting for this afternoon's press conference by King Hassan of Morocco, the chairman both of the summit meeting and of the committee appointed to see to an ending of the war. Someone remarked that we always seem to be waiting for something.

This morning at the college we had another meeting about resuming classes. Of course, it was inconclusive. Every day new people are turning up whom we haven't seen for weeks. Among others, I saw Z, who has been growing tomatoes in his backyard in the south. We laughed as he regaled me with an account of his uncharacteristic new occupation. He has been cultivating his garden, an excellent thing to do these days!

On my way home I bumped into several different groups of students, all eager to know when, and if, the semester will start. They know the answer as well as I do. "We shall have to wait and see," I tell them, "but *inshallah* soon." It is a great pleasure to see these young people, who have grown up in the war so anxious to get on with their lives.

As I passed one of the shops on my way, my attention was caught by what seemed, at first glance, to be a collection of bizarre jewelry in the window. When I stopped to get a closer look, I saw that it was a collection of shrapnel. The shop owner seemed delighted by my surprise and by the success of his joke, and laughed heartily. We exchanged pleasant greetings as if we were old friends, although I do not remember ever having seen him before.

May 31, 1989: We are still waiting. King Hassan's press conference disappointed many here because, although he said they were working on Lebanon, he did not offer any specifics on the new word in our vocabulary; *aliyat at tanfith*, the mechanism by which the resolutions of the summit committee having to do with the ending of the war should be put into effect. He offered an admonition that, should the summit's attempt fail, there would be no other and that the road after the failure would be a dark one leading no one knows where. After this dire warning, the relative relaxation and optimism of the last few days has begun to evaporate.

I have to start thinking of my travel plans but am loath to do so. All my friends know that I must leave soon to see to the publication of this book, but I feel they are glad when, in response to their questioning me directly, I say vaguely "Some time at the end of the month." I feel that I am abandoning them and will put off the decision as long as I can. I hope at least to be able to see classes begin before I go and to help sort out the confusion that will be inevitable when that time comes.

June 5, 1989: Yesterday we woke to the news that Ayatollah Khomeini had died. On streetcorners all around Ras Beirut bearded young men were hanging Iranian flags, with black mourning flags under them, and pasting posters of Khomeini all over the walls. People watched, muttering their disapproval. Banners with pictures of Khomeini and Koranic verses were also being strung across the empty streets, from building to building. Koranic verses were recited through loudspeakers, and the shops were all closed.

June 12, 1989: Another meeting at the College. Today was the day we were supposed to start, but it is out of the question.

June 18, 1989: We are in the doldrums. Nothing is happening. We are stuck in the middle of an ocean of negotiations that are, in large part conducted secretly while everyone is trying to decode the signs. Samir reads seven newspapers a day. I read hardly any, just glance at the headlines and tell him he knows no more than I.

They have been picking up the garbage, so the streets are a little cleaner. The electricity and water supplies have improved somewhat. We have hardly been to the shelter, although the other night, a bout of shelling scored a direct hit on an ammunition pile nearby. For hours we heard the explosions, and the sky was red with the fire.

We have been visiting friends that we have not seen for some time, especially those whose lives have been shattered by the recent events, having lost their homes, or, worse, members of their families. I find their courage and dignity as they pick up the pieces and try to get on with it deeply moving and, especially, their notable effort not to show their pain. Perhaps they know that their sorrow is shared by us all, and that the general pain includes the particular.

June 19, 1989: Another desultory meeting about classes. It looks more and more as though the possibility of teaching this summer will be out of the question. When I raised the question of what we would do if we can't begin in September, no one wanted to think about it. Next academic year is going to be a nightmare, catching up. There is no discussion yet about admissions; and the unasked questions of refunds, salaries, etc., hang heavy over everything.

I felt better afterward when I met some of the theater students. We have to give some thoughts to the plays they will work on next year. We will meet tomorrow to discuss possibilities.

Everybody knows by now that I will be leaving next week. I can see the anxiety when they ask why I am going and when I will be back. There is always the fear that another person is packing up. Although I am looking forward to the change, dreaming of clean streets and endless electricity, and, above all, seeing my sons, I feel also that I wish to remain here, to see this thing through with everyone.

June 23, 1989: But for Abou Abdou, things have been fairly quiet. In addition, of course, there have been several Israeli air raids and the usual sonic booms. Still, I have been able to do some shopping and visiting in preparation for my forthcoming trip.

I had a visit from some students the other day. They were suntanned and said they had been going to the beach regularly since the semi-ceasefire. With much hilarity they recounted how, at the beach the other day, crowds of people had been swimming and sunbathing when suddenly Abou Abdou started. By now, of course, everyone was quite used to it, except for one young woman who immediately leaped up, gathered her things, and ran for cover. She looked back—my young friends were watching all of this with great interest—and saw with visible amazement that no one else had moved. The sunbathers were still lying on their deck chairs and towels, and the swimmers continued to frolic in the water. She stood staring, transfixed for a few minutes by the collective indifference, and then slowly returned to her chair, reapplied her suntan oil, and lay down in the sun. The students remarked; "They can never stop us here. As soon as things get even a little better, we get on with life."

My spirits are always revived by these young people. In spite of the fact that they have grown up in the war, they are a mixed group, and Christians and Muslims of all sects enjoy each other's company without a qualm or a thought of confessional issues. Indeed, when they do mention these issues at all, they joke about them. I feel a little as though, in making this observation, I am betraying their steady refusal to be drawn into the divisions.

June 25, 1989: Two nights ago, there was a nightmarish return to the vicious shelling. Tens of shells whizzed by, crashing down a few hundred meters away. We did not go down to the shelter.

We have a major new problem: The shelter is swarming with fleas. We are trying to find someone to fumigate the place, but so far our efforts have been unsuccessful as all the exterminators we have called are closed. Someone gave us a new number today, and we will try again.

Last night there was shelling again but again we stayed at home. Samir just came back from seeing the taxi driver who will take us to Damascus on Tuesday: He says we should leave here at 2:00 A.M.

June 28, 1989: I leave tonight. As I have done every time before similar trips, I have walked through the house, consigning every detail to my memory. I know that, as soon as I am out of here, I will feel the tremendous fatigue of the last few months washing over me and will sleep and sleep. But I know also that the images of the war and of the people I have left behind will dominate my dreams in the weeks until I get back.

February, 1990: A few weeks after that last entry in my journal, our home received another direct hit. We heard the news while still abroad, but were not sure of the extent of the damage as the information that reached us was second- and even third-hand. When we returned, a ceasefire had been declared and we went to work immediately to mend the damage. The kitchen was totally destroyed, and several walls inside the flat were pockmarked by shrapnel. It took months to restore the place, and workers were in and out of the house constantly.

At first, and once again, we thought the war was over. In October, the schools and universities reopened at last, promising to make up for the time lost in the spring and summer. Members of parliament met, discussed the issues, and finally agreed on political reforms and a format for the withdrawal of Syrian troops from the country. A new president was elected, and plans for reconstruction were being prepared which included the restoration of power and water supplies. But no. Our hopes, which experience had not permitted to flower into euphoria, collapsed again. The new president was assassinated in another massive car bomb, and although a successor was immediately elected, the situation returned for some time to the familiar condition of no peace, no war. We were grateful for a few hours of electricity a day and filled up on water when it came. More people decided to leave, and those who had planned to return cancelled their reservations. Then the war began again, with fratricidal battles first in the south and now in the eastern region, and as I write East Beirut is engulfed in flames. In the meantime, the Israeli occupation in the south continues, as does the interminable series of Israeli air raids.

The question is, who is ultimately responsible for these fifteen years of war and misery? Will there some day be trials, and individuals held accountable? To what extent are the people, all of us, to bear the blame? One after the other, the partisan leaders, backed by this or that foreign power which has its own stake in the game, have been denounced as having been too willing to impose on their own people or those perceived as their enemies untold suffering in order to achieve their political or personal ambitions. Yet have not each of them had their followers, people who obeyed their orders, or, at best, tolerated their presence, falling emotional prey to the easy slogans and martial calls? Then have not many of those, though too late, seen through the deceptions and renounced their own enthusiasm? Have there not also been some truths, some ideologies or causes worth fighting for, but which have been betrayed by the very inhumanity of the war?

No doubt all this is true, yet the vast majority, whatever their sympathies, have had no direct involvement in the fighting, and see themselves and the country as victims of regional and international forces over which they have no control. They hold the world responsible, especially the great powers, both regional and global, not only for the various episodes of the war, but also for allowing, or even encouraging, the endless supply of weapons and armaments which have made it possible.

Until now punishment has been issued at random and in advance, and the price has been paid by the people on all sides. There has been no justice in this, even if the responsibility is perceived to be collective.

Several years ago, in one of the recurring attempts to restore law and order, an example was required to put fear into the hearts of ordinary criminals who were increasingly active in the anarchic conditions created by the war. They took a man and tried and condemned him for murder. He was carried, screaming and kicking, to the gallows in the public garden. The law, it seems, requires that justice to be done, must be perceived by all to have been done. There was no question of his guilt. He had confessed to the murder of his landlady and her son. He had, indeed, not only killed them, but mutilated them as well. He had cut up their bodies into small pieces in order to dispose of them. He was deranged, the police said, and had done the murders in order to settle, in his own way, the gambling debts which he owed his victims.

He screamed all the way from the prison to the gallows. He struggled and kicked his bound feet, sometimes dragging them, in his terror, unable to walk. He was carried, tied, and manacled, and the black hood was forced over his bucking head. It took five or six men to hold him down and place his neck in the noose. He screamed and kicked and struggled, and had to be held until the last twitch of his poor broken body, until the last spasm of death, as the dawn light filtered through the palm trees in the garden.

The pictures were all over the newspapers, a whole page of pictures in most of them, this spectacle of justice being done. There was hardly a murmur of protest: He wasn't much worth protesting over. He was the very dregs of a humanity as mutilated as his victims' bodies. In the middle of a cruel war, in which a hundred thousand people had already died, one pitiful, deranged man had been chosen to expiate all the crimes, and had been dragged to an ignominious death in a public garden at dawn, and this was perceived as Justice.

And it was a kind of justice, in a world without justice, that Justice should be thus represented.

Today, we continue to speculate about the future, seeing several alternatives ahead. One, which we have always dreaded as *at-taqsim* (the partition) and never really believed would happen, but which looms before us now as a possibility, is the final split-up of the country into two, or into several, cantons which would separate the major religious communities. Another possibility is a continuation of today's situation for years more, with months of calm interrupted by periods of fighting, until the Palestine question, of which the war in Lebanon has been a part, is settled. The war would continue, and more and more destruction would ensue.

But the outcome the vast majority of people continue to hope for is the restoration of total peace, with the various regions of the country and their people open to each other, the barriers and barricades removed forever, with justice and dignity, and without the corruption, injustices, and decadence of the past. The militias would be dissolved, but the political parties to which they belong, representing a variety of viewpoints, would continue to exist, flourishing in the healthy climate of dialogue. Freedom of thought and speech would be given a new impetus, and Beirut, chastened by its experience— cleaned, rebuilt and with a new beauty—would become again an important regional center, its vitality given over to productive ventures, contributing to the development of the entire area and the accomplishment of justice in it. It is on this hope that we continue to build our lives, in spite of the difficulties.

VIII

Beirut:
An Alphabet

ONE of the greatest sources of pride in Beirut has been the frequently affirmed claim that the alphabet, which provides language with a controlling order, was invented here in ancient times. Thus, all human advances since are traceable to their bright beginning in this location. Yet it is here that order has been so terribly threatened. In the last years of war, although the state and its institutions came close to collapsing, total social chaos was somehow averted. Perhaps this is due to the momentum of thousands of years of history and civilization, the same source from which the alphabet arose.

Is it possible to hope that from the rubble of the war, which at certain times seemed to have ended civilization, a new form might arise and permit future creativity? There is something of the alpha and omega in this hope, is there not?

Zbale	*garbage surrounds us, everywhere we look, there are piles of rubbish, debris, there is stench and ugliness, we*
Yield	*always we yield to the force of things, we are in danger of surrendering to despair, and to the ease of*
Xenophobia	*there is always someone else to blame for what has happened to us, it's never our fault, oh no, and meanwhile we are*
Waiting	*always waiting, for the others, for the solution, waiting for them to let the water come gurgling into our empty taps, waiting for the walls to crumble*
Weary	*of the never ending*
War	*we listen, overwhelmed with sorrow and anger to the empty*
Words	*the endless empty rhetoric which has only brought more*
Violence	*while the*
Veneer	*of fashion glitters like a worthless, forgotten coin in a mound of rubble as it catches the sun.*
Ugliness	*surrounds us, the ugliness of a broken city, ugly buildings sprouting up everywhere, ugly streets, whole neighborhoods, the beauty of mountains is destroyed by utilitarian ugliness, and*
Time	*weighs heavily on us—our days are long, and*

	we carry History on our backs, an intolerable burden—but History gave us also
Tyre	*and*
Tripoli	*and*
Sidon	*timeless relics from the past, ancient, beautiful, but*
Scarred	*by war and the suffering of*
Refugees	*We are a land of refugees, a people of refugees, coming from everywhere, going nowhere.*
Refugees	*make beautiful causes, but they are people— their trucks piled high with the pathetic remnants of former lives, mattresses and goats and children and stoves—they have found no*
Quarter	*because this place is like*
Quicksand	*in which everyone sinks. We are in a*
Prison	*of violence and forgotten ideals. Still,*
Peace	*will come, and*
Oppression	*will end, must end, and*
Nemesis	*will come, but not with more*
Militias	*certainly not with more fighting men, nor with more*
Lies	*the lies told by everyone to preserve the war and to prevent the*
Knitting	*together of the unravelling whole.*
Justice	*In war there is no Justice, and it is not from War that Justice will come.*

Jbeil	*ancient Byblos, and*
Jounieh	*with its ancient harbors and stunning bay, emerald mountains dipping into the blue sea and reaching into the azure skies, they are in danger of drifting away from us, but someday perhaps there will be*
Joy	*and*
Jubilation	*when this war ends and the*
Internecine	*butchery ends. They say*
Hope	*springs eternal and so it does, in spite of the*
Guns	*and the*
Fawda	*the anarchy which threatens us at every turn, because*
Earth	*around us is beautiful: the gray rocks on the sheer cliffs, the shimmering silver leaves of the olive trees, the deep dark green of the ancient cedars, the sweet smell of the pine forests, the oranges dotted like yellow stars in the sparkling groves that lie by the blue seas. Meanwhile, our*
Days	*pass, drearily, with explosions shattering the stillness of the nights. Our senses are dulled by the*
Catastrophe	*that has been upon us here in*
Beirut	*—poor, ugly, stricken Beirut, broken Beirut, unloved city, lost Beirut, like the child in the tale, torn between two mothers, but no Solomon here, no true mother.*
Beirut	*pleads to be redeemed, but not by*

Another

Army.

ABOUT THE AUTHOR

Jean Said Makdisi was born in Jerusalem and educated in English schools in Cairo and at Vassar College. She remained in the United States for more than ten years beyond college, returning to the Middle East, to Beirut, in 1972. Ms. Makdisi is married and the mother of three sons, all raised during the war. Presently, she teaches English and Humanities at Beirut University College.

DATE DUE

APR 14 2009	

GAYLORD	PRINTED IN U.S.A.